# EMERGENCY

❦

# PREPAREDNESS
# 101

# EMERGENCY

# PREPAREDNESS
# 101

## DEANNA BALDWIN

ARPress
ILLUMINATING IDEAS,
EMPOWERING VOICES.

**ARPress**
45 Dan Road Suite 5
Canton MA 02021
Hotline:              1(888) 821-0229
Fax:                  1(508) 545-7580

Ordering Information:
Quantity sales. Special discounts are available on quantity purchases by corporations, associations, and others. For details, contact the publisher at the address above.

Printed in the United States of America.

ISBN-13:          Softcover      979-8-89356-819-6
                  eBook          979-8-89356-820-2

Library of Congress Control Number: 2024605237

# DEDICATION

This book is dedicated in loving memory of my dad Wayne Bilyard 07/03/1944-11/30/2012 and my mom Carrol Bilyard. Thank you both for being my best friends, my rock and for always loving and encouraging me to follow my dreams.

In this book we cover various topics related to emergency preparedness, survival skills, and basic first aid. Here's a summary of the key points:

**1. Emergency Preparedness:**

Food Storage and Shelf Life:

Store a variety of non-perishable foods.

Rotate stock to maintain freshness.

Be aware of shelf life and expiration dates.

Water Storage:

Store an adequate supply of water.

Consider water purification methods.

Regularly check and replace stored water.

First Aid:

Maintain a well-equipped first aid kit.

Include essential items like bandages, antiseptics, and medications.

Consider the specific medical needs of family members.

Communication Devices:

Have reliable communication devices like radios.

Consider HAM radios for longer-range communication.

Survival Techniques:

Learn basic self-defense techniques.

Understand how to handle encounters with wildlife.

Know how to build a fire and shelter.

Butchering:

Learn how to butcher animals for food.

Understand the basic steps for butchering chickens, deer, and other animals.

Survival Skills:

Know how to collect rainwater.

Learn fire-starting techniques without matches or lighters.

Understand how to make cordage in a survival situation.

Security:

Reinforce windows and doors.

Consider the use of traps for home defense.

Herbs as Medicinal Alternatives:

Be cautious and consult professionals before using herbs as alternatives.

Some herbs have traditional uses for various health concerns.

Homemade Fishing Pole:

Create a makeshift fishing pole using a flexible branch, fishing line, and a hook.

Learn how to clean and fillet fish.

Emergency Plan:

Identify potential risks in your region.

Create a communication plan and emergency kits.

Define evacuation routes and shelter-in-place procedures.

Assign responsibilities and practice regularly.

Document the plan and share it with each family member.

Remember, these are general guidelines, and it's crucial to adapt them to your specific circumstances and seek professional advice where needed. Preparedness and knowledge are key components of successfully navigating emergency situations.

## 2. Create a Basic Emergency Kit:

Food and Water: Stockpile non-perishable food and water for at least three days.

First Aid Kit: Include basic medical supplies and any necessary prescription medications.

Flashlights and Batteries: Ensure you have a reliable light source.

Communication Devices: Have a battery-powered or hand-crank radio for updates.

## 3. Develop a Communication Plan:

Establish a plan for reaching family members in case of separation.

Share important contacts and meeting places.

## 4. Build a Financial Reserve:

Set aside some cash in case of power outages or banking disruptions.

## 5. Learn Basic Skills:

Acquire basic survival skills like first aid, fire-making, and basic self-defense.

## 6. Secure Your Home:

Reinforce doors and windows.

Consider investing in a home security system.

## 7. Stockpile Essentials:

Identify essential items you use regularly and keep a surplus (toilet paper, hygiene products, etc.).

## 8. Create a Bug-Out Bag:

Prepare a portable emergency kit in case you need to evacuate quickly.

## 9. Learn and Practice:

Regularly review and update your emergency plans.

Conduct drills with your family to ensure everyone knows what to do.

## 10. Community Engagement:

Connect with neighbors and local community groups for mutual support.

## 11. Stay Informed:

Keep informed about local and global events that may impact your area.

## 12. Document Important Information:

Keep copies of important documents (IDs, insurance, medical records) in a secure, easily accessible place.

## 13. Long-Term Preparedness:

Consider long-term preparations like gardening, learning about sustainable practices, or even off-grid alternatives.

## 14. Mindset:

**Stay calm and rational during emergencies. A positive mindset can make a significant difference.**

Remember, prepping is a personal and evolving process. Tailor your preparations to your specific circumstances and regularly update your plans as needed.

## Preppers guide to food storage, shelf life and correct food temperatures.

Proper food storage is crucial for preppers to ensure that their emergency food supplies remain safe and nutritious. Here's a guide on food storage, shelf life, and correct food temperatures:

### 1. Food Storage Basics:

Cool, Dark, and Dry: Store food in a cool, dark place away from direct sunlight and moisture.

Airtight Containers: Use airtight containers to prevent exposure to air and humidity.

Rotation System: Practice the "first in, first out" (FIFO) system to use older supplies before newer ones.

### 2. Shelf Life Guidelines:

Canned Goods: Many canned foods have a shelf life of 1-5 years or more. Check for any signs of bulging or rusting before consuming.

Dry Goods (Rice, Beans, Pasta): These items can last for several years if stored properly. Keep them in airtight containers to prevent pests and moisture.

Dehydrated and Freeze-Dried Foods: Can have a shelf life of 20 years or more if stored in optimal conditions.

Spices and Herbs: Their potency diminishes over time, so consider replacing them every 1-3 years.

### 3. Correct Food Temperatures:

Refrigerator: Keep the refrigerator at or below 40°F (4°C). Regularly check and monitor the temperature.

Freezer: Maintain a freezer temperature of 0°F (-18°C) or lower.

Hot Foods: Keep hot foods at 140°F (60°C) or above to prevent bacterial growth. Use a food thermometer to check temperatures.

### 4. Food Storage Containers:

Mylar Bags: These provide an additional layer of protection against light and oxygen for long-term storage.

Vacuum Sealing: Removes air from the packaging, extending the shelf life of many foods.

Food-Grade Buckets: Ideal for storing larger quantities of dry goods.

### 5. Labeling and Dating:

Clearly label containers with the contents and date of storage.

Regularly check and rotate perishable items to ensure freshness.

### 6. Consider Temperature Fluctuations:

Avoid temperature extremes, as they can affect the quality of stored food. For example, don't store food in a place that experiences wide temperature variations.

### 7. Inspect Regularly:

Check stored items regularly for signs of spoilage, pests, or damage to packaging.

### 8. Special Considerations:

Baby Formula and Pet Food: Follow specific storage guidelines for these items.

Medications: Store medications according to their specific requirements.

### 9. Water Storage:

Rotate water supplies regularly and use proper containers designed for long-term water storage.

### 10. Educate Yourself:

Understand the specific storage needs of different types of food items.

### 11. Plan Meals Accordingly:

Include a variety of foods with different shelf lives in your prepper food storage plan.

By following these guidelines, you can maximize the shelf life of your emergency food supplies and ensure that they remain safe and nutritious when you need them.

## How much food should you keep on hand?

The amount of food you should keep on hand depends on various factors, including the size of your household, dietary needs, storage space, and your specific goals for preparedness. Here are some general guidelines to help you determine how much food to keep on hand:

### 1. Emergency Food Supply Duration:

Start with a goal for how many days or weeks you want your emergency food supply to last. Many preppers aim for a minimum of two weeks to a month.

### 2. Household Size:

Consider the number of people in your household. Your food supply should be sufficient to meet the needs of everyone, including children, elderly family members, and pets.

### 3. Caloric Requirements:

Calculate the daily caloric needs for each person in your household. This will depend on factors such as age, gender, activity level, and health conditions.

### 4. Types of Food:

Include a variety of foods that provide essential nutrients. A balanced supply should include grains, legumes, protein sources, fruits, vegetables, and fats.

### 5. Special Dietary Needs:

Consider any special dietary needs or restrictions within your household, such as allergies or medical conditions.

### 6. Water Supply:

Ensure an adequate supply of water. The general recommendation is at least one gallon of water per person per day for drinking and sanitation.

### 7. Seasonal Considerations:

Take into account seasonal variations and potential weather-related challenges that might affect your ability to access food.

### 8. Food Rotation:

If possible, plan for a rotation system where you use and replace items regularly to avoid expiration and spoilage.

### 9. Storage Space:

Consider the available storage space in your home. Ensure that your chosen storage areas are cool, dry, and away from direct sunlight.

### 10. Culinary Versatility:

Include versatile ingredients that can be used in multiple recipes to avoid food fatigue.

### 11. Non-Perishable Foods:

Focus on non-perishable items with longer shelf lives, such as canned goods, dry goods, and freeze-dried or dehydrated foods.

### 12. Pets:

Don't forget to include food for any pets in your household.

### 13. Budget Considerations:

Balance your preparedness efforts with your budget. Start with the essentials and gradually build up your supplies over time.

### 14. Local Regulations:

Be aware of any local regulations or guidelines regarding food storage and emergency preparedness.

### 15. Regular Assessments:

Periodically reassess and update your emergency food supply based on changes in your household, needs, and available resources.

Remember that your food supply should be tailored to your specific situation and needs. It's also important to have a well-rounded emergency plan that includes other essentials, such as water, medical supplies, and communication tools.

# Eating to survive

Eating to survive, especially in emergency situations, involves making thoughtful choices to ensure you get the necessary nutrients and energy to maintain health and well-being. Here are some considerations for eating to survive:

### 1. Prioritize Nutrient-Dense Foods:

Choose foods that provide essential nutrients. Nutrient-dense options include whole grains, legumes, nuts, seeds, dried fruits, and dehydrated vegetables.

### 2. Include Protein Sources:

Protein is crucial for maintaining muscle mass and overall health. Include protein sources like canned meats, beans, lentils, and nuts.

### 3. Healthy Fats:

Incorporate sources of healthy fats, such as nuts, seeds, and oils. These provide concentrated energy and essential fatty acids.

### 4. Hydration:

Maintain proper hydration. Water is essential for survival. Ensure you have an adequate supply of clean water for drinking and sanitation.

### 5. Balance and Variety:

Strive for a balanced diet that includes a variety of food groups. This helps ensure you get a broad spectrum of nutrients.

### 6. Consider Dietary Restrictions:

If you have dietary restrictions or allergies, be mindful of choosing foods that align with your needs.

### 7. Portion Control:

Practice portion control to make your food supply last longer. Conserve resources and avoid overeating.

### 8. Long Shelf-Life Items:

Include foods with longer shelf lives, such as canned goods, dry goods, and freeze-dried or dehydrated foods.

### 9. Food Rotation:

Rotate your food supply to prevent items from expiring. Use the "first in, first out" (FIFO) system to consume older items first.

### 10. Caloric Intake:

Pay attention to your caloric intake. In survival situations, you may need to adjust your activity level and energy expenditure.

### 11. Multivitamins and Supplements:

Consider including multivitamins or essential nutrient supplements to fill potential gaps in your diet.

### 12. Cooking Alternatives:

Plan for alternative cooking methods, such as portable stoves, camping cookware, or solar cookers, depending on your situation.

### 13. Mindful Eating:

Be mindful of your eating habits. Conserve food, savor each bite, and avoid unnecessary waste.

### 14. Food Preservation:

Learn basic food preservation techniques, such as canning or drying, to extend the shelf life of perishable items.

### 15. Community Support:

If possible, connect with local communities or support networks. Sharing resources and collaborating with others can enhance your collective survival efforts.

### 16. Mental Well-being:

Consider the psychological aspect of eating. Maintaining a positive mental state is essential for overall well-being.

Remember, while these guidelines are useful for emergency situations, it's also important to have a well-rounded emergency plan that includes other essentials like water, medical supplies, and communication tools. Additionally, seek guidance from relevant authorities and experts to ensure you are adequately prepared for any survival scenario.

## Are MRE'S better to have on hand than regular food?

Whether MREs (Meals Ready-to-Eat) are better than regular food depends on the specific context, your preferences, and your preparedness goals. Here are some factors to consider when deciding between MREs and regular food:

### MREs (Meals Ready-to-Eat):
### Convenience:

MREs are designed for convenience in emergency situations. They require no cooking or preparation, making them easy to use when traditional cooking methods are not available.

### Caloric Density:

MREs are often formulated to be calorically dense, providing a significant amount of energy in a compact package. This can be beneficial in survival situations where energy needs are high.

### Long Shelf Life:

MREs have a long shelf life, often up to several years. This makes them suitable for long-term storage and emergency preparedness.

### Portability:

MREs are lightweight and portable, making them easy to carry in a bug-out bag or emergency kit.

### Complete Meals:

MREs typically contain a full meal with an entrée, side dishes, snacks, and desserts, ensuring a balanced nutritional intake.

### Regular Food:
### Taste and Variety:

Regular food often offers more variety and better taste compared to MREs. If you have the means to cook or prepare meals, you may prefer the flavor and freshness of regular food.

Cost:

Regular food is usually more cost-effective than MREs. Building a pantry with non-perishable items and rotating them as needed can be a budget-friendly approach.

## Customization:

With regular food, you have more flexibility to customize your meals based on dietary preferences, restrictions, and nutritional needs.

## Availability:

In everyday situations, regular food is more readily available and accessible. MREs are typically purchased as part of emergency preparedness supplies.

## Cooking Options:

If you have access to cooking facilities, regular food allows you to prepare meals according to your preferences and dietary requirements.

## Considerations:

Diversification:

It's often advisable to have a combination of both MREs and regular food to diversify your emergency food supply.

## Storage Space:

Consider the available storage space. MREs may be more space-efficient, while regular food may require more storage space.

## Duration of Need:

Assess the likely duration of your emergency situation. For short-term emergencies, MREs may be sufficient, but for longer-term scenarios, a combination of MREs and regular food might be more practical.

Ultimately, the best approach may involve a combination of MREs, long-lasting non-perishable foods, and fresh items if possible. It's important to regularly review and rotate your emergency food supply to ensure freshness and readiness. Additionally, consider your personal taste preferences, dietary needs, and the specific requirements of your emergency preparedness plan.

**What are the best super foods, and caloric-dense foods to keep stocked?**

Including nutrient-dense and calorie-rich foods in your emergency stockpile is crucial for sustaining energy and maintaining health. Here are some examples of superfoods and calorie-dense options to consider:

**Nutrient-Dense Foods:**

Quinoa:

A complete protein source with essential amino acids and high in fiber.

Chia Seeds:

Rich in omega-3 fatty acids, fiber, and antioxidants.

Kale:

Packed with vitamins A, C, and K, as well as calcium and antioxidants.

Blueberries:

High in antioxidants, vitamins, and fiber.

Almonds:

A good source of healthy fats, protein, and vitamin E.

Sweet Potatoes:

High in vitamins A and C, fiber, and complex carbohydrates.

Salmon (Canned):

Provides omega-3 fatty acids, protein, and various vitamins and minerals.

Broccoli:

Rich in fiber, vitamins C and K, and antioxidants.

Spinach:

High in iron, vitamins A and K, and folate.

Beans (Canned or Dried):

Excellent source of protein, fiber, and various vitamins and minerals.

**Calorie-Dense Foods:**

Peanut Butter:

High in healthy fats, protein, and calories.

Nuts (e.g., Walnuts, Pecans):

Provide healthy fats, protein, and calories.

Olive Oil:

Calorically dense with heart-healthy monounsaturated fats.

Dried Fruits (e.g., Apricots, Dates):

High in natural sugars and calories.

Coconut Oil:

Calorically dense with medium-chain triglycerides (MCTs).

Avocado:

Rich in healthy fats, providing a good source of calories.

Cheese (Hard, Shelf-Stable):

Calorie-dense and a source of protein and calcium.

Whole Milk Powder:

A convenient source of calories and essential nutrients when rehydrated.

Canned Meat (Chicken, Tuna):

Provides protein and calories in a shelf-stable form.

Granola:

Contains oats, nuts, and dried fruits, providing a mix of calories and nutrients.

General Tips:

Multivitamins and Supplements:

Consider including multivitamins to supplement potential nutrient gaps.

**Hydration:**

Alongside these foods, remember to store an adequate supply of clean water for hydration.

**Rotation and Expiration Dates:**

Regularly check and rotate your stockpile to ensure freshness. Pay attention to expiration dates.

**Individual Preferences:**

Tailor your stockpile to suit the preferences and dietary needs of your household.

**Variety**

Include a variety of foods to ensure a well-balanced diet.

Remember that these suggestions are general guidelines, and individual dietary needs may vary. Always consult with healthcare professionals or nutritionists, especially if there are specific health considerations or dietary restrictions within your household.

**How much water should you stock up on? How long is it good for?**

Water is a critical component of emergency preparedness, and the amount you should stock up on depends on several factors, including the number of people in your household, your climate, and the duration of the emergency. Here are some general guidelines:

**1. Daily Water Needs:**

The general recommendation is to store at least one gallon of water per person per day for drinking and sanitation.

Consider factors such as age, health, physical activity, and climate when determining individual needs.

**2. Household Considerations:**

Account for all members of your household, including children, elderly family members, and pets.

**3. Emergency Duration:**

Aim to have a supply that can sustain your household for at least three days to two weeks. For longer-term preparedness, consider extending to a month or more.

**4. Climate Considerations:**

Hotter climates may require a higher water intake, so adjust your stockpile accordingly.

In colder climates, you still need to stay hydrated, even if you may not feel as thirsty.

## 5. Sanitation Needs:

Remember to include water for sanitation purposes, such as hygiene and basic cleaning.

## 6. Alternative Water Sources:

If possible, identify alternative water sources such as lakes, rivers, or rainwater collection, and have appropriate purification methods available.

## 7. Water Storage Containers:

**Use food-grade containers designed for water storage.**

Consider larger containers, such as 55-gallon drums, for extended water storage.

## 8. Water Purification:

Include water purification methods (filters, tablets, or boiling) in your emergency kit.

## 9. Regular Rotation:

Regularly rotate your water supply to ensure freshness. Stagnant water can develop an off taste over time.

## 10. Check Expiration Dates:

If you're using commercially bottled water, check the expiration dates and replace as needed.

## 11. Storage Conditions:

Store water in a cool, dark place, away from direct sunlight and chemicals. Avoid storing it directly on concrete floors.

## 12. Water for Cooking:

Include water for cooking purposes in your calculations.

## 13. Community Water Sources:

Connect with your local community to identify emergency water sources and distribution points.

**14. Educate Household Members:**

Ensure that all household members are aware of the importance of water conservation.

**15. Water Needs for Special Groups:**

Consider the needs of infants, elderly family members, and individuals with special medical conditions.

**Shelf Life of Stored Water:**

**Commercially Bottled Water:**

**If stored in a cool, dark place, commercially bottled water typically has a shelf life of about two years.**

**Treated or Purified Water:**

Properly treated or purified water can last indefinitely if stored in a clean, airtight container.

Regularly assess your emergency water supply and make adjustments as needed. It's a good practice to include water in your overall emergency preparedness plan and to stay informed about water safety in your local area.

**How to safely purify water?**

Purifying water is crucial in emergency situations to ensure it is safe for consumption. Here are several methods for safely purifying water:

**1. Boiling:**

Boiling is one of the most effective methods to kill harmful microorganisms.

Bring water to a rolling boil for at least one minute (or three minutes at higher altitudes).

**2. Water Purification Tablets:**

Commercial water purification tablets, like those containing chlorine or iodine, can be used to disinfect water.

Follow the instructions on the tablet packaging for proper usage.

### 3. Water Filters:

Use water filters designed for camping or emergencies. These can remove bacteria, parasites, and some chemicals.

Follow the manufacturer's instructions for proper use and maintenance.

### 4. UV Water Purifiers:

UV (ultraviolet) purifiers use UV light to kill bacteria, viruses, and other microorganisms.

Follow the device's instructions for proper use and exposure time.

### 5. Solar Disinfection (SODIS):

SODIS involves exposing clear plastic or glass bottles filled with water to sunlight for at least six hours.

This method is effective in killing bacteria and viruses.

### 6. DIY Filtration:

Create an improvised filter using layers of clean cloth, sand, and charcoal to remove larger particles and some contaminants.

This method improves water clarity but may not eliminate all microorganisms.

### 7. Distillation:

Distillation involves boiling water and then collecting the vapor as it condenses back into liquid.

This process removes contaminants that do not vaporize.

### 8. Chlorine Bleach:

Unscented and pure chlorine bleach can be used for water disinfection.

**Add 8 drops of bleach per gallon of water, mix, and let it stand for 30 minutes before using.**

### 9. Iodine Solution:

Iodine can be used for water disinfection. **Add 5 drops of 2% tincture of iodine per quart of clear water (or 10 drops for cloudy water).**

Let it stand for 30 minutes before drinking.

- Portable water purification straws have built-in filters and can be used to drink directly from water sources.

Important Tips:

**Pre-Filtering:**

Pre-filter water with a cloth or fine mesh to remove debris before using purification methods.

**Clear Instructions:**

Always follow the manufacturer's instructions for water purification devices.

**Water Source Selection:**

Whenever possible, choose the clearest water source available to reduce the burden on purification methods.

**Regular Maintenance:**

If using filters, UV purifiers, or other devices, regularly clean and maintain them according to the manufacturer's guidelines.

**Emergency Water Storage:**

If drawing water from stored sources, ensure that the containers are clean and properly sealed.

Remember that water purification methods are often most effective when used in combination. For example, you might pre-filter water, then use boiling or chemical treatment for thorough purification. Tailor your approach based on the available resources and the specific contaminants present in the water source.

**Where can I buy water purification tablets? How do I use them?**

Water purification tablets are commonly available at outdoor and camping supply stores, as well as in the camping or emergency preparedness sections of larger retail stores. You can also find them online through various retailers.

**Here are steps on how to use water purification tablets:**

Buying Water Purification Tablets:

Outdoor and Camping Stores:

Retailers specializing in outdoor and camping gear often carry water purification tablets.

Examples include REI, Cabela's, or local outdoor equipment stores.

Online Retailers:

Websites like Amazon, Walmart, and other online retailers offer a wide selection of water purification tablets.

Pharmacy or Health Stores:

Some pharmacy or health stores may carry water purification tablets in their travel or first aid sections.

Preparedness and Survival Stores:

Stores that focus on emergency preparedness or survival gear are likely to have water purification tablets.

## Using Water Purification Tablets:

### Read the Instructions:

Carefully read and understand the instructions provided by the manufacturer. Different brands may have varying dosage and usage instructions.

### Select the Right Dosage:

Tablets usually come in different strengths, and the dosage may depend on water clarity. Follow the manufacturer's recommendations for dosage based on water conditions.

### Use a Clean Container:

Fill a clean container with the water you want to purify. If the water is murky, pre-filter it through a cloth or fine mesh to remove debris.

### Add the tablets:

Drop the prescribed number of tablets into the water. Be sure not to touch the tablets with your bare hands to avoid contamination.

**Wait for the Required Time:**

Allow the tablets to dissolve and take effect. The waiting time varies depending on the brand and specific product. Common waiting times are around 30 minutes, but it can be longer for certain tablets.

**Stir or Shake (if required):**

Some tablets may require you to stir or shake the water after adding them. Check the instructions for any specific mixing requirements.

**Check for Discoloration:**

After the required waiting time, visually check the water for any discoloration or unusual odor. If there are concerns, it's advisable to use additional purification methods or choose a different water source.

**Taste Considerations:**

Some water purification tablets may leave an aftertaste. If this is a concern, consider using additional methods like flavor additives or filtering.

**Use Purified Water:**

Once the purification process is complete, the water is safe to drink.

**Important Notes:**

**Storage:**

Store water purification tablets in a cool, dry place, and check their expiration date regularly.

**Pregnancy and Medical Conditions:**

If you are pregnant or have specific medical conditions, consult with a healthcare professional before using water purification tablets.

**Alternative Methods:**

Water purification tablets are just one method. Consider having multiple purification methods in your emergency kit for versatility.

**Follow Local Guidelines:**

In certain emergency situations, local authorities may provide guidance on water purification methods. Follow their recommendations if available.

Always prioritize safety and follow the instructions provided by the specific brand of water purification tablets you choose.

**What should you have in your first aid kit and why? How many first aid kits should you keep on hand?**

A well-equipped first aid kit is an essential component of any emergency preparedness plan. The contents of a first aid kit can vary based on individual needs, the size of your household, and potential risks. Here's a general list of items to consider including in your first aid kit and some guidance on the number of kits to keep on hand:

**Basic First Aid Kit Contents:**

**Adhesive Bandages:**

For covering minor cuts and abrasions.

**Sterile Gauze Pads and Bandages:**

To dress larger wounds and promote healing.

**Adhesive Tape:**

Used to secure dressings in place.

**Antiseptic Wipes:**

For cleaning wounds and preventing infection.

**Tweezers:**

To remove splinters or debris from wounds.

**Scissors:**

For cutting tape, gauze, or clothing if necessary.

**Disposable Gloves:**

To protect against infection when giving first aid.

**Pain Relievers:**

Such as acetaminophen or ibuprofen for pain relief.

**Antihistamines:**

For allergic reactions and relief from allergy symptoms.

**Thermometer:**

To monitor body temperature.

**Instant Cold Packs:**

For treating sprains, strains, or reducing swelling.

**Elastic Bandages:**

To support strained muscles or joints.

**CPR Mask:**

For administering CPR safely.

**First Aid Manual:**

To provide guidance on administering first aid.

**Emergency Blanket:**

Provides warmth in case of exposure to cold weather.

**Burn Ointment:**

For treating minor burns.

Eye Wash Solution:

For flushing out foreign objects from the eyes.

**Prescription Medications:**

Any necessary prescription medications for household members.

Additional Items for Special Consideration:

**EpiPen (Epinephrine Auto-Injector):**

**For individuals with severe allergies.**

**Inhaler:**

**For individuals with asthma.**

**Medications for Chronic Conditions:**

Include medications and supplies for managing chronic conditions.

**Personal Emergency Information:**

A list of emergency contacts, medical history, and allergy information, blood type.

Number of First Aid Kits:

**Home:**

Have at least one comprehensive first aid kit for your home, easily accessible to all family members.

**Car:**

Keep a smaller, portable first aid kit in your car for emergencies that may occur while traveling.

**Workplace:**

If applicable, have a basic first aid kit at your workplace.

Specialized Kits:

Consider specialized kits for outdoor activities, such as camping or hiking, tailored to the specific risks associated with those activities.

**Number of Household Members:**

Consider the size of your household. If you have a larger family, you might need additional first aid kits or a larger kit.

**Travel:**

For frequent travelers, having a compact travel-sized first aid kit is advisable.

Maintenance:

**Check and Restock Regularly:**

Periodically check the contents of your first aid kits, replace expired items, and restock any used supplies.

**Personalize Kits:**

Tailor first aid kits to the specific needs of individuals in your household, including any special medications or medical supplies.

**Education:**

Ensure that household members are familiar with the contents of the first aid kit and know how to use them. Consider taking a basic first aid course.

Having multiple first aid kits ensures that you have the necessary supplies in various locations, increasing your readiness to respond to emergencies. Customize the contents based on your household's specific health needs and potential risks.

**What every day over-the-counter medicines should you stock up on?**

Stocking up on over-the-counter (OTC) medicines for common ailments can be a practical part of your emergency preparedness plan. Here are some everyday OTC medicines that you may consider having in your medicine cabinet:

1. Pain Relief and Fever Reducers:

Acetaminophen (Tylenol): Relieves pain and reduces fever.

Ibuprofen (Advil, Motrin): An anti-inflammatory that also reduces pain and fever.

2. Allergy Medications:

Antihistamines (e.g., cetirizine, loratadine): Relieve allergy symptoms like sneezing, itching, and runny nose.

Decongestants (e.g., pseudoephedrine): Reduce nasal congestion.

3. Cough and Cold Medications:

Cough Suppressant (e.g., dextromethorphan): Suppresses coughing.

Expectorant (e.g., guaifenesin): Helps loosen mucus.

Nasal Decongestant (e.g., phenylephrine): Reduces nasal congestion.

4. Digestive Health:

Antacids (e.g., Tums, Rolaids): Relieve heartburn and indigestion.

Anti-diarrheal (e.g., loperamide): Controls diarrhea.

5. Topical Analgesics:

Pain-Relieving Cream or Gel (e.g., Bengay, Icy Hot): Provides relief for sore muscles and joints.

6. First Aid Supplies:

Hydrocortisone Cream: Relieves itching from skin irritations.

Antibiotic Ointment (e.g., Neosporin): Prevents infection in minor cuts and wounds.

7. Eye Care:

Artificial Tears: Lubricates and soothes dry eyes.

8. Oral Health:

Oral Pain Reliever (e.g., benzocaine): Temporarily numbs oral pain.

Toothache Relief Kit: Includes temporary filling material and cotton pellets for dental emergencies.

9. Sleep Aids:

Sleep Aid (e.g., diphenhydramine): Helps with occasional sleeplessness.

10. Fever Thermometer:

- An accurate digital thermometer for monitoring body temperature.

11. Menstrual Relief:

- **Menstrual Pain Reliever (e.g., ibuprofen, naproxen):** Provides relief from menstrual cramps.

12. Motion Sickness Medications:

- **Motion Sickness Tablets (e.g., dimenhydrinate):** Helpful for travel-related nausea.

13. Electrolyte Replenishment:

- **Oral Rehydration Solution:** Useful for replacing electrolytes during dehydration.

14. Medical Supplies:

- **Band-Aids (Assorted Sizes):** For minor cuts and scrapes.

- **Cotton Balls and Swabs:** For wound care.

15. Sunscreen:

broad-spectrum sunscreen with a sun protection factor (SPF) appropriate for your skin type.

**Important Considerations:**

**Expiration Dates:**

Check the expiration dates regularly and replace any expired medications.

**Individual Needs:**

Tailor your stockpile to the specific health needs of household members.

**Chronic Conditions:**

If someone in your household has a chronic medical condition, ensure an adequate supply of any OTC medications they regularly use.

**Storage Conditions:**

Store medications in a cool, dry place, away from direct sunlight.

**Consultation with Healthcare Professionals:**

Consult with healthcare professionals if you have concerns about potential interactions with existing medications or if you have specific health conditions.

It's essential to keep in mind that while having OTC medications on hand is beneficial for minor ailments, consulting with a healthcare professional for more severe or persistent health issues is important. Additionally, always follow the recommended dosage instructions on the medication packaging.

**Should you keep kerosene lamps on hand and solar powered lights on hand?**

Having alternative lighting sources in your emergency preparedness kit is a prudent decision. Both kerosene lamps and solar-powered lights offer advantages, and their appropriateness depends on your specific needs, preferences, and the nature of potential emergencies. Here are considerations for both:

**Kerosene Lamps:**

Advantages:

Reliability: Kerosene lamps can provide a reliable and consistent source of light.

Long Burn Time: Depending on the size of the lamp and the amount of kerosene stored, they can burn for an extended period.

Portability: Kerosene lamps are relatively portable and can be moved to different areas as needed.

**Considerations:**

**Ventilation:** Kerosene lamps produce fumes, so proper ventilation is crucial to prevent indoor air pollution.

**Storage:** Kerosene has a limited shelf life, so regular checks and proper storage are necessary.

**Safety:** There is a fire risk associated with kerosene lamps. Use them with caution and follow safety guidelines.

**Solar-Powered Lights:**

Advantages:

**Renewable Energy:** Solar-powered lights use renewable energy from the sun, making them an environmentally friendly option.

**Long-Term Use:** With proper care, solar lights can last for an extended period.

**No Fuel Required:** Solar lights do not require fuel, reducing the need for storage and potential safety concerns.

**Variety of Types:** Solar lights come in various forms, including lanterns, flashlights, and string lights, providing versatile lighting options.

Considerations:

Dependence on Sunlight: Solar lights rely on sunlight to charge. They may not be suitable for prolonged periods of inclement weather or limited sunlight.

**Battery Life:** Check and replace rechargeable batteries as needed for optimal performance.

**Initial Cost:** While the long-term cost is low, there may be a higher initial investment in solar-powered lights compared to some other options.

Recommendations:

Diversification:

Consider having a combination of both kerosene lamps and solar-powered lights to diversify your lighting options.

**Emergency Situations:**

In situations where extended power outages are likely, having multiple lighting sources, including both traditional and solar-powered options, can be beneficial.

**Indoor Use:**

For indoor use, especially in confined spaces, solar-powered lights may be a safer and more convenient option.

**Outdoor Use:**

Solar-powered lights are excellent for outdoor use, such as in a backyard or during camping, where there is access to sunlight for charging.

**Safety Precautions:**

Follow safety guidelines for using kerosene lamps, and be mindful of ventilation and fire safety. Additionally, store kerosene safely.

**Maintenance:**

Regularly check and maintain both kerosene lamps and solar lights to ensure they are in working condition when needed.

Ultimately, the choice between kerosene lamps and solar-powered lights depends on your specific circumstances and preferences. Having a well-rounded emergency kit that includes a variety of lighting options ensures that you are prepared for different situations.

**How long do batteries last and how should you store them?**

The lifespan of batteries can vary based on the type of battery, storage conditions, and usage patterns. Here are general guidelines for the lifespan of common types of batteries and tips for proper storage:

**Common Battery Types:**

Alkaline Batteries:

Alkaline batteries typically last 5 to 10 years in storage, depending on the conditions.

Lithium Batteries:

Lithium batteries have a longer shelf life and can last up to 15 years or more in storage.

Rechargeable NiMH Batteries:

Nickel-metal hydride (NiMH) rechargeable batteries have a shorter shelf life, typically lasting 1 to 2 years in storage.

### Tips for Battery Storage:

Cool, Dry Location:

Store batteries in a cool, dry place. Avoid exposing them to extreme temperatures, especially heat, as high temperatures can reduce battery life.

### Avoid Humidity:

High humidity can also negatively impact battery life. Keep batteries in a low-humidity environment.

### Room Temperature:

Room temperature (around 68-78°F or 20-25°C) is ideal for battery storage.

### Remove Batteries from Devices:

If devices will not be used for an extended period, remove the batteries to prevent potential leakage.

### Avoid Mixing Old and New Batteries:

When using multiple batteries in a device, try to use batteries with similar levels of charge. Mixing old and new batteries can affect overall performance.

### Charge Rechargeable Batteries Before Storage:

If you're storing rechargeable batteries, charge them before storage to prevent self-discharge over time.

### Store in Original Packaging:

If possible, store batteries in their original packaging or in a battery case to protect them from contact with other objects.

**Check Expiration Dates:**

Some batteries may have expiration dates. Be mindful of these dates, especially for alkaline and non-rechargeable batteries.

**Recharge Regularly (For Rechargeable Batteries):**

Rechargeable batteries perform best when they are used regularly. If you have rechargeable batteries in storage, consider cycling them by charging and discharging periodically.

**Use a Battery Tester:**

Periodically check the charge level of batteries using a battery tester. This helps ensure that you're using batteries with sufficient power.

Dispose of Expired Batteries Properly:

Dispose of expired or damaged batteries following local regulations. Some batteries may contain hazardous materials and should be recycled appropriately.

**Keep Battery Contacts Clean:**

Check and clean the contacts of batteries before use. Dirty contacts can reduce the efficiency of the electrical connection.

Remember that the guidelines provided are general recommendations, and actual battery life can vary based on the brand, quality, and specific conditions of use and storage. Following these tips can help maximize the lifespan and performance of your batteries.

**What communication devices should you have?**

Communication devices are crucial for staying informed and connected during emergencies. The specific devices you need may depend on your location, the nature of potential emergencies, and your personal preferences. Here are some communication devices to consider including in your emergency preparedness kit:

1. Cell Phones:

Pros: Cellular networks are widely available, providing voice and text communication.

Considerations: Ensure your phone is charged, and have a portable charger or power bank in your kit.

2. Two-Way Radios:

Pros: Ideal for short-range communication within a group.

Considerations: Choose radios with a sufficient range for your needs and ensure they are charged or have extra batteries.

3. Emergency Weather Radio:

Pros: Receives NOAA Weather Radio broadcasts for weather alerts and updates.

Considerations: Opt for a hand-crank or solar-powered model for reliability.

4. Satellite Phones:

Pros: Provides communication in remote areas where cellular networks may not be available.

Considerations: Expensive, and may require a subscription plan. Ensure it is charged and has coverage in your area.

5. Portable Wi-Fi Hotspot:

Pros: Provides internet connectivity for devices like smartphones, tablets, or laptops.

Considerations: Requires a cellular data plan. Keep it charged and have a backup power source.

6. CB Radio:

Pros: Allows communication with other CB radios in the area.

Considerations: Limited range compared to other options. Useful for short-range communication.

7. Hiking/Outdoor GPS Devices:

Pros: Useful for navigation and location tracking.

Considerations: Some models offer two-way communication features. Ensure it is charged and has updated maps.

8. Personal Locator Beacons (PLBs) or Emergency Beacons:

Pros: Sends distress signals to emergency services with your location.

Considerations: One-way communication for emergencies. Requires registration.

9. Whistle or Signal Mirror:

Pros: Non-electronic signaling devices for short-range communication.

Considerations: Useful for attracting attention in emergencies.

10. Emergency Messaging Apps:

- **Pros:** Apps like WhatsApp, Signal, or Telegram can provide communication during disasters.

- **Considerations:** Require internet connectivity. Set up in advance and have contacts added.

11. Laptop or Tablet:

- **Pros:** Can be used for accessing online information, communication, and emergency updates.

- **Considerations:** Requires a power source and internet connectivity.

12. Power Banks and Solar Chargers:

- **Pros:** Keep your electronic devices charged in case of power outages.

- **Considerations:** Ensure power banks are charged, and have a solar charger for extended use.

**Important Tips:**

Test Devices Regularly:

Regularly test your communication devices to ensure they are in working order.

Charge Devices:

Keep devices charged, and consider rechargeable batteries or alternative power sources.

Stay Informed:

Stay informed about emergency communication channels in your area and follow official guidelines.

Practice with Two-Way Radios:

If using two-way radios, practice communication within your group to ensure everyone is familiar with their use.

Create a Communication Plan:

Establish a communication plan with your family or group, including meeting points and contact information.

Remember that different emergencies may require different communication strategies. Having a combination of devices that offer various communication options can enhance your preparedness and resilience in different scenarios.

**What are HAM radios?**

HAM radios, also known as amateur radios, are two-way radios that are used by licensed operators for personal, non-commercial communication. "HAM" stands for "amateur," and HAM radio operators, often referred to as "hams," engage in radio communication as a hobby. HAM radio communication is an important part of emergency preparedness and public service, as it provides a reliable means of communication when other systems may be unavailable.

Key Features of HAM Radios:

Frequency Bands:

HAM radios operate on a variety of frequency bands, including VHF (Very High Frequency), UHF (Ultra High Frequency), and HF (High Frequency). Different bands have different propagation characteristics, allowing for communication over varying distances.

License Requirement:

**To operate a HAM radio legally, individuals must obtain an amateur radio license from their country's telecommunications regulatory authority. Licensing often involves passing an exam covering radio theory, regulations, and operating procedures.**

Wide Range of Communication:

HAM radios can communicate locally, regionally, or globally, depending on the frequency band and propagation conditions. Some bands are suitable for short-range communication within a city, while others can facilitate long-distance communication.

Diverse Modes of Communication:

HAM radios support various modes of communication, including voice (AM, FM, SSB), Morse code (CW), digital modes (such as PSK31 and FT8), and more. This versatility allows for communication under different conditions.

Emergency Communication:

**HAM radio operators often play a vital role in emergency communication. During disasters or emergencies, when other communication systems may fail, HAM radio operators can provide essential communication links for emergency services and the community.**

Community and Public Service:

**HAM radio operators frequently participate in community events, public service activities, and support local authorities during parades, marathons, and other events where reliable communication is needed.**

Equipment Variety:

HAM radio equipment comes in various forms, from handheld transceivers for local communication to mobile and base stations with higher power for longer-range communication. Antennas also vary depending on the desired frequency band and application.

Global Community:

HAM radio operators are part of a global community. They can communicate with other hams around the world, participate in contests, and exchange information on various topics.

**Why HAM Radios for Emergency Preparedness?**

Independent Infrastructure:

HAM radios operate independently of traditional communication infrastructure. They can be useful when regular communication systems are down.

Reliable Communication:

HAM radios can provide reliable communication in various conditions, including natural disasters, power outages, and other emergencies.

Community Support:

HAM radio operators often form local emergency communication groups, providing valuable support to emergency services and local communities.

Learning and Skill Development:

Becoming a licensed HAM radio operator involves learning about radio theory, regulations, and practical skills. This knowledge can be valuable in emergency situations.

While HAM radio operation requires a license, the process of obtaining a license is designed to ensure that operators understand the principles of radio communication and can use the technology responsibly. If you're interested in HAM radio, consider exploring local amateur radio clubs and resources to learn more about the licensing process and how to get started.

**Do you need a license to use a HAM radio in emergency situations?**

**In many countries, including the United States, you generally need a license to operate a HAM radio, even in emergency situations. The license is typically issued by the country's telecommunications regulatory authority and is required to ensure that operators understand the principles of radio communication, adhere to regulations, and operate their equipment responsibly.**

Licensing Requirements:

Amateur Radio License:

To legally operate a HAM radio, you need to obtain an amateur radio license. The licensing process often involves passing an exam that covers radio theory, regulations, and operating procedures.

License Classes:

Licensing may have different classes, each granting certain privileges. The specific classes and privileges can vary by country. In the U.S., for example, there are three main license classes: Technician, General, and Extra.

Frequency Bands and Modes:

The license you hold determines the frequency bands and modes you are authorized to use. Higher-level licenses often grant access to more frequency bands and operating modes.

**Emergency Communications Exception:**

**While a license is generally required for regular HAM radio operation, there is an important exception for emergency communications. In many countries, including the United States, licensed amateur radio operators are permitted to provide emergency communications without specific authorization during emergencies or disaster situations. This exception is often referred to as "emergency operations" or "emergency communications."**

Emergency Communications Privileges:

During emergency operations, licensed amateur radio operators may have expanded privileges, such as:

Cross-Band Repeater Operation:

The ability to use cross-band repeaters to extend communication range.

Temporary Operation on Restricted Frequencies:

Temporary authorization to operate on frequencies and modes that are typically restricted by their license class.

Coordination with Emergency Services:

Collaborating with emergency services and organizations to provide essential communication support.

Important Considerations:

License Requirement:

While there is an exception for emergency operations, it's important to note that this exception does not negate the overall requirement for a license during normal operation.

3Emergency Declarations:

The ability to operate without specific authorization during emergencies is often contingent on official emergency declarations by relevant authorities.

Good Samaritan Laws:

In some jurisdictions, "Good Samaritan" laws may protect licensed amateur radio operators providing emergency communications assistance during disasters.

Training and Preparedness:

Licensed HAM radio operators involved in emergency communications often undergo training and participate in drills to ensure they are well-prepared to assist in real emergency situations.

Cooperation with Authorities:

During emergencies, HAM radio operators often work in coordination with emergency services to provide additional communication support.

It's crucial for amateur radio operators to familiarize themselves with the regulations in their specific country or region, including any provisions related to emergency communications. Staying informed and participating in local emergency communication groups and drills can contribute to effective and responsible emergency communications.

**Will cellphones work if there is an EMP?**

An Electromagnetic Pulse (EMP) is a burst of electromagnetic radiation. It can be caused by natural events, such as a solar flare, or by man-made sources, such as a nuclear explosion. The potential impact of an EMP on electronic devices, including cellphones, depends on various factors, and the topic is often a subject of debate and speculation.

**Here are key points to consider regarding cellphones and EMPs:**

1. EMP Effects on Electronics:

EMPs can induce electrical currents in conductive materials, potentially damaging or destroying electronic components. The severity of the impact depends on factors like the strength and proximity of the EMP.

2. EMP Strength and Range:

High-altitude nuclear detonations can generate EMPs with a wide area of effect. In such cases, electronic devices, including cellphones, could be affected over a large geographic area.

3. Cellphone Hardening:

Some military and critical infrastructure electronic systems are designed with EMP hardening measures to reduce vulnerability. However, consumer electronics like cellphones may not have the same level of protection.

4. Likelihood of Impact:

While EMP events are a concern, the likelihood of a catastrophic EMP event causing widespread damage to electronics, including cellphones, is a subject of ongoing debate among experts. Natural EMPs from solar events are less likely to cause significant damage compared to man-made EMPs.

5. EMP Protection Devices:

There are devices and systems designed to protect electronics from EMPs. However, the effectiveness of these devices can vary, and their use for consumer electronics like cellphones is not widespread.

6. Solar Flares vs. Nuclear EMP:

The impact of EMPs from solar flares (solar storms) on cellphones is generally considered to be lower than that of EMPs generated by nuclear detonations. Solar flares are more likely to affect power grids and long-range communication systems.

7. Localized EMP vs. Global EMP:

The potential impact of an EMP is often discussed in terms of localized events (e.g., a nuclear explosion in the atmosphere) versus global events (e.g., a massive solar storm). Localized EMPs may have a more limited impact on electronic devices.

Recommendations:

Limited EMP Preparedness for Cellphones:

While EMP preparedness is a topic of interest, it is not practical or feasible for individuals to protect their cellphones from all possible EMP scenarios.

General Emergency Preparedness:

Focus on general emergency preparedness, which includes having alternative communication methods (such as two-way radios), backup power sources, and a plan for staying informed during disasters.

Solar Flare Preparedness:

In the case of potential disruptions from solar flares, emergency preparedness should include considerations for power grid failures and reliance on alternative communication methods.

Government and Infrastructure Resilience:

The resilience of critical infrastructure, including power grids and communication systems, is a key factor in minimizing the impact of EMP events. Governments and organizations are responsible for implementing measures to enhance infrastructure resilience.

In summary, the potential impact of EMPs on cellphones is complex and depends on various factors. While the risk is a consideration, it's important for individuals to focus on broader emergency preparedness measures that address a range of potential scenarios.

**What is the morse code chart?**

**Morse code is a method of encoding text characters using sequences of dots and dashes to represent the letters, numbers, and punctuation of a written message. Each letter or numeral is represented by a unique combination of dots and dashes. Here is a basic Morse code chart:**

**Morse Code Chart:**

A: ·−

B: −···

C: −·−·

D: −··

E: ·

F: ··−·

G: −−·

H: ····

I: ··

J: ·−−−

K: −·−

L: ·−··

M: −−

N: −·

**O:** ---

**P:** ·--·

**Q:** --·-

**R:** ·-·

**S:** ···

**T:** -

**U:** ··-

**V:** ···-

**W:** ·--

**X:** -··-

**Y:** -·--

**Z:** --··

**\*\*0:** -----
**\*\*1:** ·----

**\*\*2:** ··---

**\*\*3:** ·····−

**4:** ·····

**5:** −·····

**6:** −−···

**7:** −−−··

**8:** −−−−·

**9:** −−−−−

## Punctuation and Special Characters:

**.:** ·−·−·−

**,:** −−··−−

**?:** ··−−··

**":** ·−−−−·

**!:** −·−·−−

**/:** −··−·

**(:** −·−−·

**):** −·−−·−

**&:** ·−···

**;:** −·−·−·

**=:** −···−

**+:** ·−·−·

**-:** −····−

**___:** ··−−·−

**@:** ·−−·−·

**Morse Code Timing:**

In Morse code, the duration of a dot is the basic unit of time, and dashes are three times the duration of dots. The space between symbols (dots and dashes of the same letter) of the same word is one dot time, while the space between words is seven dot times.

Morse code can be transmitted by sound, light, or other means, with dots represented by short signals and dashes by longer ones.

Remember that learning Morse code involves both decoding (listening to Morse code and translating it into letters) and encoding (writing a message in Morse code). Practice is key to becoming proficient in Morse code communication.

**How much cash should you keep on hand?**

The amount of cash you should keep on hand can depend on various factors, including your spending habits, emergency preparedness needs, and personal preferences. Here are some considerations to help you determine an appropriate amount:

1. Daily Expenses:

Consider how much cash you typically use for daily expenses such as groceries, transportation, and small purchases. Having a week's worth of these expenses in cash can be a reasonable starting point.

2. Emergency Preparedness:

Emergency situations, such as power outages or natural disasters, may limit access to electronic payment methods. Having a sufficient amount of cash for emergency supplies, temporary accommodations, or other immediate needs can be crucial.

3. Local Services and Businesses:

Some local services or businesses may prefer or only accept cash. If you frequently visit such places, it might be useful to keep a small amount of cash on hand.

4. ATM Availability:

Consider the availability of ATMs in your area. If ATMs are scarce, having extra cash may be more important.

5. Travel Plans:

When traveling, especially to areas with unreliable or limited access to ATMs, having a reasonable amount of cash in the local currency can be beneficial.

6. Cash-Only Situations:

Certain situations, events, or markets may operate on a cash-only basis. If you participate in these activities, having cash on hand is necessary.

7. Financial Security:

Having a small emergency fund in cash can provide financial security in case of unexpected expenses or disruptions to regular income.

8. Personal Comfort Level:

Some individuals feel more comfortable having a larger amount of cash readily available for peace of mind. Others may rely more on digital or card-based transactions.

Important Tips:

Safe Storage:

Store your cash in a secure and accessible location. Consider a home safe or another secure option.

Regular Review:

Periodically review and update the amount of cash you keep on hand based on your needs and circumstances.

Small Denominations:

Keep a mix of small and large denominations. Small bills can be useful for everyday transactions.

Emergency Kit:

Include a small amount of cash in your emergency kit along with other essential items.

Consider Inflation:

Over time, the purchasing power of cash can be eroded by inflation. Regularly assess and adjust the amount you keep on hand to account for changes in the cost of living.

Digital Alternatives:

While having cash is important, consider utilizing digital payment methods for convenience and security.

Recommendations:

Emergency Fund:

In addition to cash on hand, maintain a more substantial emergency fund in a savings account or other liquid asset to cover larger unexpected expenses.

Local Currency:

When traveling internationally, carry a reasonable amount of the local currency to cover immediate expenses upon arrival.

Practicality:

The amount of cash you keep on hand should be practical and align with your lifestyle and financial habits.

Ultimately, the appropriate amount of cash to keep on hand is a personal decision. It's advisable to strike a balance between having enough for daily needs and emergencies while also considering security and practicality. Regularly reassess your cash needs based on changes in your circumstances.


## What is the barter system and how does it work?

The barter system is a method of exchanging goods and services directly for other goods and services without the use of money as a medium of exchange. In a barter system, individuals or entities trade items they possess for items they need, creating a system of mutual benefit. This form of trade predates the use of currency and was historically one of the primary means of conducting transactions.

### Key Features of the Barter System:

### Direct Exchange:

In a barter system, there is a direct exchange of goods or services between two parties. Each party offers something they have in surplus in exchange for something they need.

**No Intermediary (Money):**

Unlike modern economies that use money as a medium of exchange, the barter system does not involve a common currency. Instead, participants rely on the inherent value of the items being exchanged.

**Double Coincidence of Wants:**

For a barter transaction to occur, both parties must have something the other wants. This requirement is known as the "double coincidence of wants," and it can be a limitation in the barter system.

**Absence of Standardized Values:**

Unlike money, which serves as a standardized measure of value, the barter system lacks a universal measure. The value of goods and services in a barter transaction is subjective and negotiated between the parties involved.

**Limited to Localized Transactions:**

The barter system is typically more practical for localized transactions where individuals or communities have direct contact with each other.

**Example of Barter Transactions:**

Farmers Trading Goods:

A farmer with surplus vegetables might exchange them with a neighboring farmer who has an excess of eggs. Both parties benefit from obtaining items they need without using money.

Skills Exchange:

Individuals with different skills might barter services. For instance, a carpenter may exchange carpentry work for the services of a plumber.

Goods for Services:

Someone who is skilled in making handmade crafts might exchange those crafts for the services of a tutor or music teacher.

Challenges and Limitations of the Barter System:

Double Coincidence of Wants:

Finding a party with exactly what you need, who also needs what you have, can be challenging.

Lack of Standardization:

Without a standardized measure of value, determining fair exchange rates can be subjective and may lead to disagreements.

Inefficiency:

The barter system can be less efficient than monetary transactions, particularly in complex economies with a wide variety of goods and services.

Storage and Transport Issues:

Some goods may be difficult to store or transport, limiting the feasibility of barter transactions.

Divisibility:

Certain goods may not be easily divisible for smaller transactions, making it challenging to exchange them for smaller-value items.

Historical Context:

The barter system was prevalent in ancient societies where goods and services were exchanged within local communities.

As economies evolved, the limitations of the barter system led to the development of money as a more efficient medium of exchange.

**While the barter system is less common in modern economies, it can still be observed in certain situations, local communities, or as a supplement to conventional economic systems. In the absence of a common currency, individuals must negotiate and agree on the terms of each transaction based on the perceived value of the goods or services being exchanged.**

**What are the steps of self defense against an attacker?**

Self-defense is a critical skill that involves protecting oneself from harm or danger. It's important to note that self-defense should prioritize personal safety, and the goal is to escape the situation whenever possible. Here are general steps and principles to consider when practicing self-defense against an attacker:

## 1. Awareness and Avoidance:

Stay Aware: Be alert to your surroundings and potential threats. Avoid distractions like excessive phone use when in public.

Trust Your Instincts: If something feels off or makes you uncomfortable, trust your instincts and take precautionary measures.

## 2. Maintain Distance:

Create Space: Keep a safe distance from strangers, especially in isolated or dimly lit areas.

Personal Bubble: Be aware of your personal space, and if someone invades it, establish a boundary.

## 3. Verbal De-Escalation:

Stay Calm: Keep a calm demeanor and try to defuse the situation verbally.

Assertive Communication: Speak assertively, set boundaries, and make it clear that you are not comfortable.

## 4. Use Body Language:

Confident Posture: Stand tall with confident body language. Avoid appearing vulnerable or fearful.

Maintain Eye Contact: Establish and maintain eye contact to show confidence.

## 5. Self-Defense Techniques:

Target Vulnerabilities: Focus on attacking vulnerable areas, such as eyes, nose, throat, groin, and knees.

Learn Basic Techniques: Enroll in self-defense classes to learn basic techniques for escaping holds, breaking grips, and incapacitating attackers.

Use Your Body: Utilize your body's natural weapons, such as elbows, knees, and heels, in a defensive manner.

## 6. Escape and Run:

Create an Opening: If possible, create an opportunity to escape by momentarily distracting or surprising the attacker.

Run to Safety: Once there's an opening, run to the nearest safe location, such as a crowded area or a place with security.

## 7. Use Tools for Self-Defense:

Personal Alarms: Carry a personal alarm that can be activated to attract attention.

Whistle: A loud whistle can serve as a simple but effective tool for alerting others.

Self-Defense Products: Items like pepper spray or a personal safety alarm can provide an added layer of defense.

## 8. Call for Help:

Emergency Contacts: Have emergency contact numbers programmed into your phone for quick access.

Yell for Help: In a dangerous situation, yell loudly to attract attention and call for help.

## 9. Report to Authorities:

Report Incident: After escaping to safety, report the incident to law enforcement. Provide as much detail as possible.

## 10. Practice Regularly:

Training: Regularly practice self-defense techniques to build muscle memory and confidence.

Mental Preparedness: Stay mentally prepared and review safety strategies periodically.

Important Tips:

Stay Calm:

It's crucial to remain calm and focused to make effective decisions.

Practice Situational Awareness:

Being aware of your surroundings can help you identify and avoid potential threats.

Seek Professional Training:

Consider enrolling in self-defense classes taught by certified instructors to learn effective techniques.

Use Your Voice:

A loud and assertive voice can be a powerful tool for deterring attackers and attracting attention.

Cooperate if Necessary:

In some situations, compliance may be the safest option. Prioritize your safety above all else.

Remember that self-defense is a personal choice, and individuals should choose methods that align with their comfort level and abilities. Regular practice and ongoing awareness are key components of effective self-defense.

**What are the basic self-defense techniques?**

Basic self-defense techniques are practical skills that individuals can learn to protect themselves in various situations. It's important to note that these techniques are intended for personal safety and self-preservation, and the goal is to escape from a dangerous situation whenever possible. Here are some basic self-defense techniques:

**1. Palm Heel Strike:**

Execution: Use the heel of your palm to strike the attacker's nose or chin. This can be a powerful strike to create distance.

**2. Eye Gouge:**

Execution: Use your fingers to target the eyes of the attacker. Gouging the eyes can be a highly effective way to disable an assailant temporarily.

**3. Groin Kick:**

Execution: Deliver a swift kick to the attacker's groin. This can incapacitate the assailant and create an opportunity to escape.

**4. Knee Strike:**

Execution: Lift your knee and strike the attacker's groin or midsection. This is effective at close range.

## 5. Elbow Strike:

Execution: Use your elbow to strike the attacker's face, throat, or other vulnerable areas. Elbow strikes are powerful and can be executed at close quarters.

## 6. Escape from Holds:

Wrist Grab Escape: Rotate your wrist to loosen the grip and pull away.

Bear Hug Escape: Stomp on the attacker's foot and strike the head with your elbow to break free.

## 7. Palm Escape:

Execution: If someone grabs your wrist, use your opposite hand to press against the thumb, creating space to pull away.

## 8. Choke Defense:

Front Choke Defense: Use the "pluck and strike" technique to break the grip and counter-attack.

Rear Choke Defense: Drop your weight, step to the side, and strike the attacker before escaping.

## 9. Basic Strikes:

Jab: Use your front hand to quickly jab at the attacker's face to create distance.

Cross Punch: Follow a jab with a cross punch for added impact.

## 10. Basic Ground Defense:

- **Guard Position:** If on the ground, assume a guard position to protect your face and create space.

- **Escape and Get Up:** Learn techniques to escape from the ground and get back on your feet.

## 11. Use of Everyday Objects:

- **Keys:** Use keys as a makeshift weapon by holding them between your fingers.

- **Pen:** A pen can be used for striking vulnerable areas.

## Important Tips:

Practice Regularly:

Consistent practice is crucial for building muscle memory and confidence in executing self-defense techniques.

Focus on Vulnerable Areas:

Target areas such as eyes, nose, throat, groin, and knees, as they are vulnerable and can incapacitate an attacker.

Use Your Voice:

Shout loudly to attract attention and deter the attacker.

Escape:

The primary goal is to create an opportunity to escape. Once safe, seek help and report the incident.

Stay Aware:

Situational awareness is key. Be aware of your surroundings and potential threats.

Seek Professional Training:

Consider enrolling in self-defense classes taught by certified instructors to learn and practice techniques effectively.

Remember that self-defense is a personal choice, and individuals should choose methods that align with their comfort level and abilities. The key is to stay prepared, be aware of your surroundings, and prioritize your safety.

## What is the basic escape and get up techniques?

Basic escape and get-up techniques are essential components of self-defense, especially when dealing with situations where you find yourself on the ground. These techniques are designed to help you create distance from an attacker, regain your footing, and improve your chances of escaping safely. Here are some basic escape and get-up techniques:

## 1. Guard Position:

Execution:

Lie on your back with your feet on the ground and knees bent.

Keep your hands up to protect your face, with your elbows close to your body.

## 2. Elbow Escape (from Guard):

Execution:

Use one arm to push against the attacker's hip while keeping the other arm protecting your face.

Create space and slide your knee inside, pushing the attacker's leg away.

Use the space to escape and get back on your feet.

## 3. Shrimp Escape (from Side Control):

Execution:

Turn to your side and use your bottom leg to push against the ground.

Create space by moving your hips away (shrimping).

Recover guard position or stand up.

## 4. Technical Stand-Up:

Execution:

From a seated position, place one foot forward and the other foot back.

Use your hands to post on the ground and lift your hips.

Stand up by bringing the back foot forward.

## 5. Knee Recovery (from Side Control):

Execution:

Turn to your side and use your bottom arm to frame against the attacker's hip.

Bring your bottom knee up toward your chest.

Recover to a kneeling position and stand up.

## 6. Granby Roll (from Turtle Position):

Execution:

From a turtle position (hands and knees), tuck your head and roll over your shoulder.

Use the momentum to create space and stand up.

## 7. Front Kick Get-Up:

Execution:

If an attacker is standing over you, use a front kick to create distance.

Quickly move to a seated position and then stand up.

## 8. Back Kick Get-Up:

Execution:

If an attacker is behind you, use a back kick to create space.

Quickly turn to face the attacker and stand up.

## 9. Technical Get-Up (from Ground and Pound):

Execution:

When an attacker is on top throwing strikes, protect your face with one arm.

Use the other arm and the same-side leg to create a frame.

Create space, shrimp away, and work back to your feet.

## Important Tips:

Practice Regularly:

Consistent practice of these techniques is essential for developing muscle memory.

Use Momentum:

Many escape techniques involve using your body's natural movements and momentum.

Stay Calm:

Remaining calm and focused will improve your ability to execute techniques effectively.

Combine Techniques:

Combine different escape and get-up techniques based on the specific situation you find yourself in.

Adapt to Circumstances:

Adapt the techniques based on the surface you are on (e.g., hard ground, soft ground).

Seek Professional Instruction:

Consider seeking guidance from a qualified self-defense or martial arts instructor to learn and practice these techniques in a controlled environment.

Remember, the primary goal of these techniques is to create an opportunity to escape and seek help. Prioritize your safety, and use these techniques as part of an overall self-defense strategy.

**How to use your keys in self-defense?**

Keys can be used as makeshift self-defense tools in emergency situations. When using keys for self-defense, the goal is to create an opportunity to escape from a potentially dangerous situation. Here are some techniques for using keys in self-defense:

**1. Key Grip:**

Execution:

Hold the keys in your hand with one or more keys protruding between your fingers.

Create a tight fist with the keys extending outward, forming a pointed edge.

**2. Eye Jab:**

Execution:

Aim for the attacker's eyes.

Use a jabbing motion with the key hand to strike the eyes and face.

**3. Neck Strike:**

Execution:

Aim for vulnerable areas, such as the side or back of the attacker's neck.

Use a slashing or jabbing motion to strike these areas.

**4. Face Strike:**

Execution:

Target the attacker's face, particularly the nose and mouth.

Use quick and forceful strikes to create an opportunity to escape.

## 5. Groin Strike:

Execution:

Aim for the attacker's groin area.

Use a thrusting or jabbing motion to create distance.

## 6. Ear Strike:

Execution:

Strike the side of the attacker's head, targeting the ears.

Use a quick, forceful motion to disorient the attacker.

## 7. Knee Strike:

Execution:

Target the attacker's knees, particularly the side or back of the knee joint.

Use a slashing or jabbing motion to disrupt the attacker's balance.

## 8. Palm Strike:

Execution:

Use the keys in a clenched fist for a palm strike to the attacker's face.

Aim for the nose, throat, or other vulnerable areas.

## 9. Combination Strikes:

Execution:

Combine key strikes with other self-defense techniques, such as kicks or palm strikes, to increase effectiveness.

Important Tips:

Prioritize Safety:

Use key strikes as a means to create an opportunity to escape, not to engage in prolonged confrontation.

Practice Technique:

Practice key strikes in a controlled environment to build confidence and improve accuracy.

Maintain Awareness:

Stay aware of your surroundings and potential threats while using key strikes.

Seek Professional Guidance:

Consider seeking guidance from a self-defense instructor to learn and practice key strikes effectively.

Use Force as a Last Resort:

Key strikes should be used as a last resort when escape is not immediately possible.

Report the Incident:

After using key strikes to escape, report the incident to the authorities.

Remember that self-defense situations are dynamic, and the use of keys should be approached with caution and within the bounds of the law. It's essential to prioritize your safety, remain calm, and seek help immediately after creating an opportunity to escape.

**What is the guard position in self-defense?**

The guard position is a defensive posture used in self-defense, particularly in situations where you find yourself on the ground facing an attacker. The guard position is commonly associated with martial arts and self-defense systems, including Brazilian Jiu-Jitsu and Krav Maga. It allows you to protect your vital areas, create space, and work towards regaining control or standing up. Here's a basic explanation of the guard position:

Basic Guard Position:

Lie on Your Back:

Begin by lying on your back on the ground.

Bend Your Knees:

Bend your knees, placing your feet flat on the ground. Your feet should be shoulder-width apart.

Protect Your Face:

Bring your hands up to protect your face. Your elbows should be close to your body.

Closed Guard:

If possible, close your guard by bringing your legs up and crossing your ankles. This helps to control the distance between you and the attacker.

Open Guard:

In an open guard, your legs are not crossed. Instead, you use your legs to create distance and control the attacker.

Purpose of the Guard Position:

Protection: The guard position provides a protective barrier for your face and vital areas, reducing the risk of direct strikes.

Control: By closing or opening your guard, you can control the distance between you and the attacker, limiting their ability to strike or advance.

Escape Opportunities: The guard position allows for movement and maneuverability, creating opportunities to escape from the ground.

Techniques from the Guard Position:

Armbar:

If the attacker reaches in, you may attempt an armbar by securing control of their arm and hyperextending the elbow.

Triangle Choke:

From the closed guard, you can attempt a triangle choke by trapping the attacker's head and arm using your legs.

Sweeps:

Sweeps involve off-balancing the attacker to create an opportunity to reverse the position or stand up.

Important Tips:

Stay Mobile:

While in the guard position, stay mobile and use your legs to create angles and openings.

Breathe:

Keep a steady breathing pattern to maintain composure and energy.

Escape Safely:

Look for opportunities to escape and stand up when it's safe to do so.

Adapt to the Situation:

Adapt your guard position based on the circumstances, the attacker's movements, and the environment.

Practice Regularly:

Regularly practice guard position techniques to build muscle memory and improve effectiveness.

Considerations:

The guard position is just one aspect of ground-based self-defense. Depending on the situation, you may need to transition to other positions or techniques to ensure your safety.

Seeking professional instruction from a qualified self-defense or martial arts instructor is advisable for learning and practicing guard position techniques in a controlled environment.

Remember that the goal of the guard position is to provide a defensive and strategic posture while looking for opportunities to escape or gain control of the situation.


**What do you do if you encounter wildlife?**

Encountering wildlife can be a fascinating experience, but it's essential to approach such situations with caution and respect for the animals. Your actions may vary depending on the type of wildlife you encounter. Here are some general guidelines for dealing with wildlife encounters:


**1. Stay Calm:**

Remain calm and avoid sudden movements. Do not run, as this may trigger a chase response in certain animals.

**2. Assess the Situation:**

Determine the type of wildlife and its behavior. Some animals may be more defensive or aggressive, especially if they feel threatened or have offspring nearby.

### 3. Give Them Space:

Back away slowly and give the wildlife plenty of space. Respect their territory and avoid cornering them.

### 4. Avoid Direct Eye Contact:

Direct eye contact can be perceived as a threat. Keep your gaze averted and use your peripheral vision to monitor the animal's behavior.

### 5. Make Noise:

If you're in an area known for wildlife, consider making noise to alert animals to your presence. This can help avoid surprising them.

### 6. Do Not Feed Wildlife:

Feeding wildlife can alter their natural behaviors, make them dependent on human food, and pose risks to both the animals and humans.

### 7. Protect Yourself:

If you are in an area with potentially dangerous wildlife (e.g., bears, big cats), carry bear spray or other appropriate deterrents. Know how to use them effectively.

### 8. Back Away Slowly:

If the wildlife seems agitated, slowly back away without turning your back to them. Maintain a safe distance.

### 9. Stay in Groups:

When hiking or exploring, stay in groups. Larger groups are often perceived as more intimidating by wildlife.

### 10. Do Not Approach or Touch:

- Never approach or attempt to touch wildlife. Maintain a respectful distance to ensure both your safety and the animal's welfare.

### 11. Stay on Trails:

- Stick to designated trails to minimize the impact on wildlife habitats and reduce the chances of surprise encounters.

### 12. If Attacked:

- If a wild animal attacks, do your best to protect your vital areas, play dead if appropriate (e.g., for a bear attack), and fight back if necessary.

### 13. Report Unusual Behavior:

- If you observe wildlife behaving unusually or see injured animals, report it to local wildlife authorities or park rangers.

### 14. Know Local Wildlife:

- Familiarize yourself with the types of wildlife in the area you are visiting. Knowing their habits and behaviors can help you react appropriately.

### 15. Keep Pets Leashed:

- If you have pets with you, keep them on a leash to prevent them from approaching or provoking wildlife.

### 16. Follow Regulations:

- Adhere to any regulations or guidelines provided by local authorities regarding wildlife encounters.

### 17. Educate Yourself:

- Take wildlife awareness courses or seek information about local wildlife behaviors and safety precautions.

### 18. Leave No Trace:

- Practice "Leave No Trace" principles to minimize your impact on wildlife and their habitats.

### 19. In Water Encounters:

- Exercise caution in areas where wildlife may be present, especially in bodies of water. Some animals may be more defensive near their nests.

Remember that wildlife encounters are unique, and responses may vary based on the species involved. Always prioritize your safety and the well-being of the animals. If you are unsure about how to handle a specific wildlife encounter, seek guidance from local wildlife experts or park rangers.

### What do you do if you are attacked by wildlife?

Being attacked by wildlife is a rare but serious situation that requires quick thinking and appropriate action to minimize harm. The specific steps you should take depend on the type of wildlife involved. Here are general guidelines for responding to wildlife attacks:

## 1. Stay Calm:

Try to remain as calm as possible. Panic can escalate the situation.

## 2. Assess the Situation:

Identify the type of wildlife and its behavior. Different animals may require different responses.

## 3. Do Not Run:

Running away can trigger a chase response in many animals, including predators. Stand your ground and avoid turning your back on the animal.

## 4. Make Yourself Look Bigger:

If you're dealing with a large mammal like a bear or a big cat, raise your arms to make yourself appear larger. Open your jacket or hold it above your head if possible.

## 5. Back Away Slowly:

Back away slowly without making sudden movements. Maintain eye contact with the animal, but do not stare aggressively.

## 6. Avoid Direct Eye Contact:

In the case of large predators, direct eye contact can be perceived as a threat. Use your peripheral vision to monitor their behavior.

## 7. Speak Calmly:

Speak to the animal in a calm, low voice. This may help convey that you are not a threat.

## 8. Protect Your Vital Areas:

If the animal attacks, protect your vital areas, such as your neck and abdomen, by using your arms and hands.

## 9. Play Dead (For Bears):

If you are attacked by a grizzly bear, playing dead may be the best strategy. Lie flat on your stomach with your hands clasped behind your neck and your legs spread to make it harder for the bear to flip you over.

### 10. Fight Back (For Cougars and Other Predators):

- If you are attacked by a cougar or other predatory animal, fight back aggressively. Use any available tools, such as rocks or sticks, to fend off the attacker.

### 11. Use Bear Spray (For Bears):

- If you have bear spray, use it as a deterrent. Aim for the face of the bear.

### 12. Retreat to a Safe Place:

- If possible, retreat to a safe place such as a building, vehicle, or elevated platform.

### 13. Seek Medical Attention:

- After the attack, seek medical attention immediately. Even seemingly minor injuries can lead to infections.

### 14. Report the Incident:

- Report the incident to local wildlife authorities or park rangers. Provide details about the attack to assist with wildlife management.

### 15. Prevent Future Encounters:

- Learn from the experience and take precautions to avoid future wildlife encounters. Follow guidelines for wildlife safety in the area.

Important Tips:

Know Your Surroundings:

Be aware of the wildlife that inhabits the area you are visiting. Know their habits and behaviors.

Carry Deterrents:

In areas with potentially dangerous wildlife, carry deterrents such as bear spray, and know how to use them effectively.

Travel in Groups:

When hiking or exploring, travel in groups. Larger groups are often perceived as more intimidating by wildlife.

Stay Informed:

Stay informed about wildlife activity in the area and any recent encounters reported by others.

Remember that wildlife attacks are rare, and preventive measures can significantly reduce the risk. If you're uncertain about how to handle a specific wildlife encounter, seek guidance from local wildlife experts or park rangers.

### What are basic first aid methods?

Basic first aid methods are essential skills that can help you provide initial care to someone who is injured or experiencing a sudden illness. While these techniques are not a substitute for professional medical care, they can make a significant difference in ensuring the well-being of the injured person until professional help arrives. Here are some basic first aid methods:

### 1. Assess the Situation:

Ensure the safety of yourself, the injured person, and bystanders. Assess the scene for any potential dangers.

### 2. Check Responsiveness:

Approach the person and gently tap their shoulder while asking, "Are you okay?" Check for responsiveness.

### 3. Call for Help:

If the person is unresponsive or if the injury is severe, call emergency services immediately (e.g., 911 in the United States).

### 4. Open the Airway:

If the person is unconscious, gently tilt their head backward and lift the chin to open the airway. Check for breathing.

### 5. Perform Rescue Breaths and CPR:

If the person is not breathing, begin rescue breaths and chest compressions according to CPR guidelines.

### 6. Control Bleeding:

Use a clean cloth or bandage to apply pressure to a wound to control bleeding. Elevate the injured area if possible.

## 7. Treat for Shock:

If the person is in shock (pale, sweaty, weak), have them lie down, elevate their legs slightly, and cover them with a blanket.

## 8. Immobilize Injuries:

Immobilize fractures or dislocations by using splints or bandages to prevent further injury.

## 9. Apply Cold Compress:

Use a cold compress or ice pack to reduce swelling and pain in minor injuries, such as sprains or bruises.

## 10. Remove Foreign Objects:

- If there is an object embedded in a wound, do not remove it. Instead, stabilize the object and seek professional medical help.

## 11. Administer Epinephrine (for Anaphylaxis):

- If someone is experiencing a severe allergic reaction (anaphylaxis), use an epinephrine auto-injector if available and prescribed.

## 12. Provide Comfort and Reassurance:

- Offer comfort and reassurance to the injured person. Keep them calm and encourage them to remain still.

## 13. Keep the Person Warm:

- If the person is cold or exposed to the elements, keep them warm by covering them with a blanket.

## 14. Stay with the Person:

- Stay with the injured person until professional help arrives. Monitor their condition and be prepared to provide additional assistance.

## 15. Administer Basic Medications:

- If the person has a known medical condition and carries prescribed medications (e.g., asthma inhaler, nitroglycerin), assist them in taking the medication.

## Important Tips:

Prioritize Safety:

Ensure the safety of yourself and the injured person before providing first aid.

Do No Harm:

Follow the principle of "do no harm" and only provide care within the scope of your training.

Stay Calm:

Keep a calm and composed demeanor to reassure the injured person.

Seek Professional Help:

Always seek professional medical help for serious injuries or illnesses.

Continuous Monitoring:

Continuously monitor the person's condition and update emergency services with any changes.

Know Your Limits:

Know when to seek professional help and do not attempt interventions beyond your training.

It's highly recommended to take a basic first aid and CPR course to acquire proper training and certification. These courses are often offered by organizations like the American Red Cross or local health agencies. The knowledge gained from such courses can empower you to respond effectively in emergency situations.


**How to you do CPR on an adult or child?**

Cardiopulmonary resuscitation (CPR) is a life-saving technique used in emergencies when someone's heartbeat or breathing has stopped. CPR involves chest compressions and rescue breaths to circulate blood and oxygen throughout the body. Here are the general steps for performing CPR on an adult or child:

For Adults and Children (Puberty Onward):

**1. Check for Responsiveness:**

Tap the person and shout loudly, "Are you okay?" Check if they respond. If there is no response, the person is unresponsive.

## 2. Call for Help:

If you're alone, call emergency services (e.g., 911 in the United States) or ask someone nearby to call. If a defibrillator is available, use it as soon as possible.

## 3. Open the Airway:

Tilt the person's head backward and lift the chin to open the airway. Check for breathing. If they are not breathing or only gasping, start CPR.

## 4. Perform Chest Compressions:

Kneel beside the person.

Place the heel of one hand on the center of the chest (usually between the nipples).

Place the other hand on top of the first and interlock the fingers.

Position yourself with your shoulders directly over your hands.

Use your upper body weight to compress the chest at least 2 inches (5 centimeters) deep and at a rate of 100-120 compressions per minute.

Allow the chest to fully recoil between compressions.

## 5. Rescue Breaths:

After 30 compressions, give two rescue breaths.

Pinch the person's nose shut, make a complete seal over their mouth with yours, and give a breath that makes their chest rise visibly.

Continue with chest compressions and rescue breaths in a ratio of 30:2.

## 6. Continue CPR:

Continue CPR until:

Professional help arrives.

The person starts breathing on their own.

You are too exhausted to continue.

For Children (1 Year to Puberty):

## 1. Check for Responsiveness:

Tap the child and shout loudly, "Are you okay?" Check if they respond. If there is no response, the child is unresponsive.

## 2. Call for Help:

If you're alone, call emergency services (e.g., 911 in the United States) or ask someone nearby to call. If a defibrillator is available, use it as soon as possible.

## 3. Open the Airway:

Tilt the child's head backward and lift the chin to open the airway. Check for breathing. If they are not breathing or only gasping, start CPR.

## 4. Perform Chest Compressions:

Use the same technique as for adults with modifications for a child:

Use one or two hands (depending on the child's size).

Compress the chest at least one-third the depth of the chest (about 2 inches or 5 centimeters).

## 5. Rescue Breaths:

After 30 compressions, give two rescue breaths.

Use a breath that makes the child's chest rise visibly.

Continue with chest compressions and rescue breaths in a ratio of 30:2.

## 6. Continue CPR:

Continue CPR until:

Professional help arrives.

The child starts breathing on their own.

You are too exhausted to continue.

Important Tips:

Use an AED if Available:

If an automated external defibrillator (AED) is available, follow the device's instructions and attach it as soon as possible.

Compression Quality:

Focus on providing high-quality chest compressions with adequate depth and recoil.

Rotate Compressors:

If there are multiple rescuers, rotate compressors every 2 minutes to maintain effectiveness.

Reassess Regularly:

Periodically reassess the person's condition and adjust your actions accordingly.

Stay Calm:

Stay calm and focused, and remember that any attempt at CPR is better than no attempt.

Remember, the goal of CPR is to maintain blood flow to vital organs until professional medical help arrives. It's crucial to seek professional training in CPR to ensure you are confident and capable in an emergency situation. Regularly refreshing your CPR skills through training courses is essential for staying prepared.

**How to perform the Heimlich maneuver on an adult or child?**

The Heimlich maneuver, also known as abdominal thrusts, is a first aid technique used to help clear a foreign object (such as food or an object) from a person's airway when they are choking. It involves applying quick, upward pressure to the abdomen to force the obstruction out. Here are the steps for performing the Heimlich maneuver on an adult or child:

For Adults and Children:

**1. Assess the Situation:**

Determine if the person is truly choking. Look for signs of distress, difficulty breathing, and the inability to speak or cough.

**2. Ask Permission:**

Before providing assistance, ask the person if they are choking and if they need help.

**3. Position Yourself Behind the Person:**

Stand or kneel behind the person and let them know you are going to help.

## 4. Place Your Arms Around the Person:

For an adult:

Place your arms around the person's waist.

Make a fist with one hand and place the thumb side against the middle of the person's abdomen, above the navel and below the ribcage.

Grasp your fist with your other hand.

For a child:

Kneel down and place the child in a standing position.

Adjust your position to be at the child's chest level.

Perform the Heimlich maneuver as described for adults.

## 5. Perform Abdominal Thrusts:

Deliver quick, upward thrusts to the abdomen using your hands:

Use a quick, upward motion, as if you are trying to lift the person off the ground.

Perform the thrusts in a series of five.

Check the person's mouth for the obstructing object between each thrust.

## 6. Continue Until the Object is Expelled or Help Arrives:

Continue the series of abdominal thrusts until the object is expelled, the person can breathe, or professional medical help arrives.

## 7. If the Person Loses Consciousness:

Lower the person gently to the ground.

Call emergency services (e.g., 911 in the United States) and start CPR.

Important Tips:

Be Aware of the Force Used:

Apply enough force to dislodge the object but avoid excessive force that could cause injury.

Do Not Hesitate to Call for Help:

If the person cannot breathe or speak, or if the obstruction is not cleared, call emergency services immediately.

Stay Calm and Reassure the Person:

Reassure the person that you are there to help and stay calm during the process.

Alternate with Back Blows:

If abdominal thrusts are not effective or for infants, alternate with back blows.

For Infants (Under 1 Year):

For infants, the Heimlich maneuver is not recommended. Instead, the technique involves back blows and chest thrusts:

### 1. Hold the Infant Face Down:

Place the infant face down on your forearm, holding their head and jaw with your hand.

### 2. Deliver Back Blows:

Use the heel of your free hand to deliver five back blows between the infant's shoulder blades.

### 3. Check for Object:

After back blows, check the infant's mouth for the obstructing object.

### 4. Perform Chest Thrusts:

If back blows do not clear the obstruction, turn the infant face up and perform chest thrusts.

Place two fingers on the center of the infant's chest just below the nipple line and compress the chest about 1.5 inches (4 centimeters).

### 5. Repeat Until the Object is Expelled:

Continue with back blows and chest thrusts until the object is expelled, the infant can breathe, or professional medical help arrives.

Remember to seek professional medical attention after performing the Heimlich maneuver, even if the obstruction is cleared, to ensure the person's well-being. It's important to receive proper training in first aid, including choking response, to perform these techniques effectively and safely.

## How do you successfully build a fire in a survival situation?

Building a fire in a survival situation is a crucial skill that can provide warmth, cook food, and serve as a signaling method for rescue. Success in building a fire depends on understanding the principles of fire building and having the right materials. Here's a step-by-step guide to successfully build a fire in a survival situation:

### 1. Choose a Safe Location:

Select a safe and open location for your fire away from dry grass, overhanging branches, or anything else that could catch fire.

### 2. Gather Materials:

Collect three types of materials: tinder, kindling, and fuel.

Tinder: Dry, fine materials that easily catch fire. Examples include dry leaves, grass, bark shavings, or cotton balls soaked in petroleum jelly.

Kindling: Small sticks or twigs that ignite easily and sustain the initial flame. Collect a range of sizes, from pencil-thin to finger-thick.

Fuel: Larger pieces of wood that sustain the fire once it's established.

### 3. Prepare the Fire Pit:

Clear a small area for your fire pit. Dig a shallow depression to contain the fire, and surround it with rocks to prevent the fire from spreading.

### 4. Build the Fire:

Place a small amount of tinder in the center of the fire pit.

### 5. Create a Tinder Nest:

Create a small, loose ball or nest of tinder in the center. This will be the ignition point for your fire.

### 6. Arrange Kindling:

Surround the tinder nest with a teepee or log cabin arrangement of kindling. Leave gaps for air circulation, which is crucial for combustion.

### 7. Light the Tinder:

Use a fire starter, waterproof matches, or a lighter to ignite the tinder in the center of the nest. Blow gently to encourage the flames.

### 8. Feed the Fire:

As the kindling ignites, gradually add larger sticks and twigs. Start with smaller pieces and progress to larger ones as the fire grows.

### 9. Add Fuel Logs:

Once the fire is established, add larger fuel logs to keep it burning steadily. Position the logs to allow air to flow and maintain the fire.

### 10. Maintain the Fire:

- Continue to add fuel as needed to keep the fire going. Monitor the fire to prevent it from spreading and to ensure it serves its purpose.

### Important Tips:

### Use Dry Materials:

Ensure that your tinder, kindling, and fuel are dry. Wet materials are challenging to ignite.

Gather More Materials Than You Think You Need:

It's better to have too much material than too little. Collect extra tinder, kindling, and fuel before starting.

Consider Wind and Ventilation:

Be aware of wind direction and speed. Place the fire downwind of your shelter to avoid smoke inside.

Build a Windbreak:

If it's windy, build a small windbreak with rocks or other materials to protect the fire.

Be Patient:

Allow the fire to build gradually. Rushing can lead to mistakes and wasted resources.

Know Local Regulations:

Familiarize yourself with local regulations regarding fires, especially in wilderness areas. Follow Leave No Trace principles.

Extinguish the Fire

When you're done with the fire, extinguish it completely by pouring water on it and stirring the ashes.

Building a fire in a survival situation requires practice and adaptability. Knowing how to use various fire-starting methods and being resourceful with available materials will increase your chances of success. Always prioritize safety and be aware of the environmental impact of your fire.

**How to start a fire without a lighter or matches?**

Starting a fire without a lighter or matches is a valuable survival skill. There are various methods using natural materials and techniques to create fire. Here are several methods you can use:

**1. Fire Starter Kits:**

Carry a fire starter kit containing tools such as flint and steel, magnesium fire starter, or ferrocerium rod. These kits are compact and reliable.

**2. Bow Drill Method:**

The bow drill method involves creating friction between a spindle and a fire board to generate heat. You'll need a bow, spindle, fire board, and a socket.

Make a bow by stringing a piece of cord between two ends of a curved stick.

Create a divot in the fire board and place a tinder bundle underneath.

Use the bow to rapidly spin the spindle in the divot, creating friction and heat.

Once you see smoke, transfer the glowing ember to the tinder bundle and blow gently to start a flame.

**3. Hand Drill Method:**

Similar to the bow drill, the hand drill method creates friction with your hands.

Use a spindle and fire board, but instead of a bow, twirl the spindle rapidly between your palms.

Transfer the ember to the tinder bundle and blow gently to start a flame.

**4. Flint and Steel:**

Strike a piece of flint with a steel striker to create sparks.

Aim the sparks at a tinder bundle to ignite it.

## 5. Magnifying Glass or Lens:

Use a magnifying glass or any clear lens to focus sunlight onto tinder.

Hold the lens above the tinder, adjusting the angle until the concentrated sunlight creates a flame.

## 6. Solar Method:

Use a reflective surface such as a mirror or shiny metal to direct sunlight onto tinder.

Adjust the angle until the concentrated sunlight creates a flame.

## 7. Chemical Reactions:

Certain chemical reactions can generate heat and start a fire. Potassium permanganate and glycerin is one example.

Mix a small amount of potassium permanganate with glycerin, and it will ignite.

## 8. Fire Plough:

Use a dry, soft piece of wood as a plough and another piece of wood as a base.

Push the plough back and forth along the base to create friction and generate heat.

The accumulated dust can catch fire and be transferred to a tinder bundle.

## Important Tips:

## Prepare Your Materials:

Gather dry and fine tinder materials, such as dry leaves, grass, or bark, before attempting to start a fire.

Use the Right Technique:

Choose a method that suits your skills and the materials available in your environment.

Practice:

Practice these techniques in a controlled environment before relying on them in a survival situation.

Be Patient:

Fire starting can be challenging, especially with primitive methods. Be patient and persistent.

Maintain Safety:

Be aware of fire safety and environmental considerations. Ensure the fire is under control and fully extinguished when you're finished.

Having a combination of fire-starting methods in your skill set increases your chances of success in various conditions. Always prioritize safety and environmental responsibility when starting fires in the wilderness.

**How do you make a bow and drill, how do you use it?**

The bow drill is a primitive fire-starting method that involves creating friction between a spindle and a fire board to generate heat. Here's a step-by-step guide on how to make and use a bow drill to start a fire:

Materials Needed:

Spindle:

Select a straight, dry, and non-resinous stick. Ideally, it should be about the length of your forearm.

Fire Board (Hearth Board):

Choose a dry, flat piece of wood. It should be harder than the spindle wood to create friction. Cut a small depression (or hearth) near the edge of the board.

Bow:

Use a flexible, non-resinous stick for the bow. The bowstring can be made from a shoelace, paracord, or any other strong, non-stretchy material.

Socket:

The socket provides downward pressure on the spindle. It can be a stone, a piece of hardwood, or even a second piece of wood.

Tinder Bundle:

Prepare a tinder bundle made of dry, fine materials like leaves, grass, or bark.

Steps to Make and Use a Bow Drill:

## 1. Prepare the Spindle:

Carve the spindle to be roughly cylindrical with a point at one end.

## 2. Prepare the Fire Board:

Carve a small depression (hearth) in the fire board near the edge. This is where the spindle will create friction.

## 3. Create the Bow:

Choose a flexible stick for the bow. String it with the bowstring, making sure it is tight when the bow is flexed.

## 4. Assemble the Bow Drill Set:

Place one end of the spindle in the hearth and the other end into the socket.

## 5. Hold the Bow:

Hold the bow with one hand and press it against the fire board. The spindle should fit into the hearth depression.

## 6. Apply Downward Pressure:

Place the socket on top of the spindle, applying downward pressure. This keeps the spindle in the hearth depression and helps generate friction.

## 7. Start Bowing:

Begin moving the bow back and forth rapidly. The spindle should spin in the hearth, creating friction and generating heat.

## 8. Collect the Ember:

After some time, you'll see smoke. Continue bowing until you have a glowing ember in the hearth.

## 9. Transfer the Ember:

Carefully transfer the ember to the prepared tinder bundle. Gently blow on the ember to encourage it to ignite the tinder.

10. Build the Fire:

- Once the tinder ignites, carefully transfer it to a fire pit surrounded by kindling and fuel wood. Gradually build up the fire.

Important Tips:

Wood Selection:

Choose dry, non-resinous wood for the spindle and fire board. Hardwoods are generally better for creating friction.

Consistent Pressure:

Maintain consistent downward pressure on the spindle with the socket.

Bow Technique:

Bow steadily and consistently. Rapid, even strokes are more effective than erratic movements.

Practice:

The bow drill method requires practice to master. Spend time perfecting your technique in a controlled environment before relying on it in a survival situation.

Be Patient:

Building a fire with a bow drill takes time and patience. Don't get discouraged if it doesn't work immediately.

Remember, successful use of the bow drill method requires skill and practice. It's important to be familiar with the technique and to use proper materials to increase your chances of success in a survival situation.

## How to build a proper shelter in a survival situation, what are the best things to use?

Building a proper shelter is a critical skill in a survival situation, providing protection from the elements and helping maintain body temperature. The type of shelter you build will depend on the environment, available materials, and your specific needs. Here are general guidelines and some common types of shelters you can build:

General Shelter Building Tips:

Location:

Choose a location that offers natural protection, such as under a tree, against a rock face, or in an area with natural windbreaks.

Consider the Elements:

Take into account the prevailing wind direction, potential flooding, and exposure to the sun when selecting a shelter location.

Materials:

Use natural materials in the environment, such as branches, leaves, grass, and bark. If available, use a tarp, space blanket, or other man-made materials.

Insulation:

Insulate the shelter from the ground using leaves, pine needles, or other materials to prevent heat loss.

Size:

Build a shelter that is just large enough for you to lie down comfortably. A smaller space is easier to heat with your body.

Ventilation:

Ensure proper ventilation to prevent condensation inside the shelter. Leave a small opening for air circulation.

Common Types of Shelters:

Lean-To Shelter:

Materials:

Long branches, a ridgepole, and smaller branches for roofing.

Construction:

Prop a long branch against a sturdy object at a 45-degree angle to create a sloping roof.

Place smaller branches against the ridgepole to form a roof.

Add leaves, grass, or other debris for insulation.

A-Frame Shelter:

Materials:

Two long branches for the sides, a ridgepole, and smaller branches for roofing.

Construction:

Position two long branches in an A-shape and secure them together at the top with a ridgepole.

Add smaller branches for roofing and insulation.

Debris Hut Shelter:

Materials:

Long branches for the frame, a ridgepole, and a thick layer of leaves, grass, or debris for insulation.

Construction:

Create a framework with long branches, making a tunnel-like shape.

Place a ridgepole along the top.

Cover the frame with a thick layer of leaves and debris for insulation.

Tarp Shelter:

Materials:

Tarp or space blanket, paracord or rope.

Construction:

Tie one end of the tarp to a tree or create a ridgeline using paracord.

Secure the other end to the ground using stakes or by tying it to low branches.

Pull the sides of the tarp down and secure them with stakes or rocks.

Snow Cave (For Snowy Environments):

Materials:

Snow, a shovel, and a digging tool.

Construction:

Dig into a snowbank to create an entrance.

Dig out an interior chamber large enough to lie down comfortably.

Create a raised sleeping platform inside for insulation.

Important Tips:

Stay Dry:

Ensure your shelter protects you from rain, snow, and wind. Stay dry to prevent hypothermia.

Stay Visible:

Use bright materials or create signals to make your shelter visible to rescuers.

Be Resourceful:

Use whatever materials are available in your environment. Improvise with natural or man-made items.

Test Your Shelter:

Before relying on a shelter in a survival situation, practice building it in a controlled environment to identify any issues.

Building an effective shelter requires adaptability and creativity based on your specific circumstances. Regular practice and experience will enhance your ability to build shelters quickly and efficiently in various environments.

**What is cordage? How do you make it in a survival situation?**

Cordage refers to any type of string, rope, or twine made by twisting or braiding together fibers or materials. In a survival situation, having strong and durable cordage is essential for various tasks, such as building shelters, creating tools, and securing items. While modern cordage can be brought along, it's important to know how to make it from natural materials in the wild. Here's a basic guide on making cordage in a survival situation:

Materials for Cordage:

Plant Fibers:

Stalks, leaves, or roots of certain plants can provide strong fibers. Examples include nettles, yucca, milkweed, dogbane, and cedar.

Bark:

The inner bark of certain trees, like cedar or willow, can be peeled and processed into cordage.

Animal Fibers:

Animal sinew, tendons, or intestines can be processed into cordage. For example, deer sinew or gut can be used.

Steps to Make Cordage:

### 1. Harvesting Materials:

Collect plant fibers, bark, or animal fibers. Choose materials that are long, flexible, and strong.

### 2. Processing Plant Fibers:

For plant fibers, strip away any leaves or outer layers to access the strong inner fibers.

If using bark, peel off the outer bark to expose the inner layers.

### 3. Twisting or Braiding:

Gather a bundle of fibers and twist them together to create a single strand.

For a stronger cord, twist multiple strands together in the opposite direction (counter-twist).

Alternatively, braid fibers together for added strength.

### 4. Splicing:

If the fibers are short, splice them together by overlapping the ends and twisting or braiding them into each other.

### 5. Wetting (Optional):

Dampen the fibers slightly if they are brittle. This can make them more flexible and easier to work with.

### 6. Set Length and Thickness:

Determine the length and thickness of the cordage based on your needs. Continue twisting or braiding until you achieve the desired length.

### 7. Secure Ends:

Tie knots or secure the ends of the cordage to prevent unraveling.

### 8. Testing:

Test the strength of your cordage by pulling on it gently. If it holds up, it's ready for use.

Tips for Making Cordage:

Choose the Right Materials:

Select fibers that are long, flexible, and strong. Experiment with different plants and materials to find what works best in your environment.

Twist in the Opposite Direction:

For added strength, twist individual strands together in the opposite direction (counter-twist).

Use Natural Adhesives (Optional):

In some cases, natural adhesives like pine resin or plant sap can be used to bind fibers together.

Practice:

Cordage making is a skill that improves with practice. Experiment with different techniques and materials to become proficient.

Combine Different Materials:

Combine plant fibers with animal sinew or use a combination of materials to create stronger cordage.

Learning to make cordage from natural materials is a valuable skill in survival situations. It allows you to create the tools and structures necessary for your survival using resources from the environment.

### What is the Dakota fire?

The Dakota fire pit, also known as the Dakota fire hole, is a type of fire pit designed for efficient and low-profile cooking or heating in a survival or camping setting. It consists of two holes—one for the fire and another for air intake. The design is believed to have Native American origins, particularly from the Dakota people. Here's how to construct a Dakota fire pit:

Steps to Build a Dakota Fire Pit:

### 1. Dig Two Holes:

Dig two holes side by side. The first hole, the fire hole, is for the actual fire. It should be roughly cone-shaped, wider at the bottom and narrower at the top. The second hole, the air hole, is dug at an angle to connect to the base of the fire hole.

## 2. Connect the Holes:

Connect the two holes by digging a short tunnel from the base of the fire hole to the side of the air hole. This tunnel allows air to flow into the base of the fire, promoting better combustion.

## 3. Light the Fire:

Place your tinder and kindling in the fire hole and light the fire. The design of the pit enhances airflow, resulting in a more efficient burn.

## 4. Control the Flame:

Adjust the intensity of the flame by covering or uncovering the air hole. Covering the air hole reduces the amount of oxygen, making the fire burn more slowly.

Advantages of the Dakota Fire Pit:

Efficient Combustion:

The design promotes efficient combustion by drawing in air from below the fire, allowing for a hotter and cleaner burn.

Low Profile:

The Dakota fire pit is relatively low to the ground, making it less visible from a distance. This can be advantageous in a survival or camping scenario where you may want to keep a low profile.

Reduced Smoke:

Because of the efficient combustion, the Dakota fire pit tends to produce less smoke compared to an open fire. This can be helpful in situations where minimizing visibility is important.

Wind Resistance:

The design helps protect the flames from the wind, making it a more reliable option in windy conditions.

Minimal Environmental Impact:

The small size and efficient burning of the Dakota fire pit can result in less impact on the surrounding environment compared to larger, less controlled fires.

Considerations:

Safety:

Always practice fire safety, and ensure the fire is completely extinguished before leaving the site.

Local Regulations:

Be aware of and adhere to any local regulations or guidelines regarding fires in the area where you are camping or surviving.

Leave No Trace:

Follow Leave No Trace principles by minimizing your impact on the environment and leaving the site as you found it.

The Dakota fire pit is a practical and efficient option for cooking or heating in outdoor settings, particularly in situations where minimizing visibility, reducing smoke, and conserving resources are priorities.

What else can you use from home to start a fire successfully without a lighter or matches?

In a survival situation, if you don't have access to a lighter or matches, you may need to rely on alternative methods to start a fire. Here are some household items that you can use to successfully start a fire:

Magnifying Glass or Lens:

Use a magnifying glass, eyeglasses, or any other clear lens to focus sunlight onto tinder. Hold the lens above the tinder and adjust the angle until the concentrated sunlight creates a flame.

Steel Wool and Battery:

Touching fine-grade steel wool to the terminals of a battery can create sparks. Once the steel wool begins to smolder, transfer it to your tinder to start a fire.

Flint and Steel:

If you have a piece of flint and steel, you can create sparks by striking the steel against the flint. Aim the sparks at your tinder to ignite it.

Fire Starter Kits:

If you have a fire starter kit containing tools like a ferrocerium rod or magnesium fire starter, use them to generate sparks or shavings to ignite your tinder.

Potassium Permanganate and Glycerin:

A chemical reaction between potassium permanganate and glycerin can produce heat and ignite tinder. Mix a small amount of potassium permanganate with glycerin to initiate the reaction.

Doritos or Corn Chips:

The oil content in certain snack foods like Doritos or corn chips can be used as a fire starter. Place the chips among your tinder and use a spark or flame to ignite them.

Lint from Dryer:

Lint collected from your dryer's lint trap is highly flammable. Place a small amount of lint among your tinder and use a spark or flame to ignite it.

Cotton Balls and Petroleum Jelly:

Coat cotton balls with petroleum jelly (Vaseline). The petroleum jelly helps the cotton ignite more easily and burn longer.

Aluminum Foil and Battery:

Touching aluminum foil to the terminals of a battery can create sparks. Use the sparks to ignite your tinder.

Char Cloth:

Char cloth is cotton fabric that has been charred in the absence of oxygen. It catches sparks easily and can be used to ignite tinder.

Dryer Flint:

Some types of lighters have a built-in flint that can be removed and used to create sparks when struck with steel.

Remember, it's essential to practice these methods in a safe and controlled environment before relying on them in a survival situation. Additionally, always prioritize safety and be aware of your surroundings and any potential fire hazards.

**What is the best way to secure your home without a security system?**

Securing your home without a security system involves a combination of practical measures to deter potential intruders and enhance the safety of your property. Here are several effective ways to secure your home without relying on a security system:

Improve Lighting:

Ensure good exterior lighting around your home. Motion-activated lights, especially near entrances, can deter intruders and make your property less appealing as a target.

Reinforce Doors and Windows:

Install solid doors with deadbolt locks. Reinforce door frames, and consider using longer screws for hinges and strike plates.

Install window locks and reinforce glass windows with security film or laminates.

Secure Sliding Doors:

Place a rod or piece of wood in the track of sliding glass doors to prevent them from being forced open.

Install Security Cameras:

Even if you don't have a full security system, visible security cameras can act as a deterrent. You can use dummy cameras if you're on a budget.

Maintain Landscaping:

Trim bushes and trees near windows and entrances to eliminate hiding spots for potential intruders. A well-maintained landscape makes your property less attractive to burglars.

Use Timers for Lights:

Set timers on interior lights to give the appearance that someone is home, especially when you're away. This can create the illusion of occupancy.

Get to Know Your Neighbors:

Establish a good relationship with your neighbors. Neighbors who look out for each other can be an effective deterrent and can quickly report any suspicious activity.

Secure Air Conditioning Units:

If you have window air conditioning units, secure them properly to prevent them from being easily removed.

Lock Gates and Fences:

Keep gates and fences locked to restrict access to your property. This can make it more challenging for intruders to enter.

Install Door Viewers (Peepholes):

Install peepholes in exterior doors so you can see who is outside before opening the door.

Use Window Coverings:

Keep blinds or curtains closed at night to prevent potential intruders from seeing into your home.

Secure Valuables:

Keep valuable items out of sight from windows. If burglars can't see items worth stealing, they may be less motivated to break in.

Create the Illusion of Occupancy:

Leave a radio or TV on when you're away to create noise that suggests someone is home.

Invest in Quality Locks:

Upgrade locks to high-quality deadbolt locks. Reinforce door frames to withstand forceful entry attempts.

Educate Family Members:

Teach family members about home security practices, such as always locking doors and windows, and being cautious about sharing information on social media.

Establish a Home Security Routine:

Develop a routine for checking doors, windows, and the overall security of your home before leaving or going to bed.

While these measures can significantly enhance your home's security, it's important to note that no security measure is foolproof. Combining multiple strategies provides a more comprehensive approach to securing your home without a dedicated security system.

**How do you reinforce your windows and doors?**

Reinforcing windows and doors is an important aspect of home security. Here are specific steps you can take to reinforce your windows and doors:

Reinforcing Windows:

Install Window Locks:

Use key-operated locks or window pin locks to secure sliding windows. These prevent the window from being forced open.

Use Window Security Film:

Apply security film to windows. This transparent layer holds glass together, making it more difficult for intruders to break through.

Install Window Bars or Grilles:

Window bars or grilles can be effective in preventing forced entry. Choose designs that allow for quick release in case of an emergency, such as a fire.

Upgrade to Laminated Glass:

Laminated glass consists of layers of glass with a protective interlayer. This makes it more resistant to breaking, reducing the chances of forced entry.

Reinforce Window Frames:

Ensure that window frames are strong and in good condition. Repair or replace any damaged frames promptly.

Add Window Pinning Devices:

Pinning devices prevent sliding or double-hung windows from being lifted out of their tracks. These devices can be inserted into the window frame to restrict movement.

Secure Basement Windows:

Basement windows are often vulnerable. Use window well covers to prevent unauthorized access.

Consider Window Alarms:

Install window alarms that sound when the window is opened. These can act as both a deterrent and an alert system.

Reinforcing Doors:

Install Deadbolt Locks:

Use deadbolt locks with at least a one-inch throw on exterior doors. Reinforce the strike plate with longer screws to anchor it into the door frame.

Use Reinforcement Plates:

Install reinforcement plates (security strike plates) with longer screws to strengthen the area around the lock and hinges.

Upgrade to Smart Locks:

Smart locks provide additional security features and can be controlled remotely. Some models include built-in alarms and tamper alerts.

Install Door Viewers (Peepholes):

A door viewer allows you to see who is outside before opening the door. Choose a wide-angle viewer for better visibility.

Reinforce Door Frames:

Strengthen door frames by using longer screws in the hinges and strike plates. Consider reinforcing the frame with metal plates.

Use Security Bars or Braces:

Security bars or braces can prevent a door from being forced open. These devices are typically placed at the base of the door.

Upgrade to Solid Doors:

Solid wood or metal doors are more resistant to forced entry than hollow-core doors. Ensure doors are of high-quality materials.

Install Door Alarms:

Door alarms can be placed on exterior doors to alert you if they are opened. These can be standalone devices or part of a larger security system.

Secure Sliding Doors:

For sliding glass doors, install a bar or rod in the track to prevent the door from being forced open.

Use Hinge Security Pins:

Replace standard hinges with security hinges or hinge pins. These prevent the removal of the door by preventing the removal of the hinge pin.

Remember to regularly inspect and maintain your window and door security measures to ensure they remain effective over time. Additionally, consider consulting with a professional for advice on specific security enhancements for your home.

## What essential items should I stockpile the most of?

Stockpiling essential items is a wise preparedness measure for various situations, including natural disasters, emergencies, or disruptions in supply chains. The specific items you should stockpile can vary based on your location, personal needs, and potential risks. Here's a general list of essential items to consider:

Food and Water:

Water:

Aim for at least one gallon of water per person per day for a minimum of three days. Consider water purification methods or tools.

Non-Perishable Food:

Stock canned goods, dry goods, and non-perishable items with a long shelf life. Include items like rice, pasta, beans, canned vegetables, and canned proteins.

Snacks:

Include snacks like energy bars, nuts, dried fruits, and crackers for quick and easy consumption.

Medical Supplies:

First Aid Kit:

Include bandages, antiseptic wipes, pain relievers, prescription medications, and other basic medical supplies.

Prescription Medications:

Stock an extra supply of essential prescription medications for chronic conditions.

Over-the-Counter Medications:

Include common medications for pain, fever, allergies, and stomach issues.

Hygiene and Sanitation:

Personal Hygiene Products:

Stock toiletries such as toothpaste, soap, shampoo, and feminine hygiene products.

Sanitation Supplies:

Include toilet paper, hand sanitizer, wet wipes, and garbage bags.

Clothing and Bedding:

Clothing:

Have durable and weather-appropriate clothing, including extra socks, underwear, and outerwear.

Blankets and Sleeping Bags:

Provide warmth and comfort in case of power outages or displacement.

Shelter and Tools:

Tarp and Plastic Sheeting:

Useful for emergency shelter or covering damaged areas.

Multi-Tool:

A versatile tool for various tasks.

Lighting and Communication:

Flashlights and Batteries:

Ensure you have reliable sources of light.

Battery-Powered or Hand-Crank Radio:

Stay informed about the latest developments and emergency alerts.

Cooking and Food Preparation:

Portable Stove or Camp Cookware:

Allows for cooking without relying on electricity.

Manual Can Opener:

Essential for accessing canned goods.

Financial and Important Documents:

Cash:

Have some cash on hand in case of power outages or electronic payment system failures.

Important Documents:

Keep copies of important documents such as identification, insurance policies, and medical records in a waterproof container.

Miscellaneous:

Fire Extinguisher

For small fire emergencies.

Entertainment and Comfort Items:

Include books, games, or other items to keep spirits up during challenging times.

Face Masks and Gloves:

Especially relevant during health emergencies.

Remember to regularly check and rotate stockpiled items to ensure they remain within their expiration dates. Customize your stockpile based on your family size, specific needs, and any unique circumstances in your area. Additionally, consider creating a family emergency plan and staying informed about potential risks in your region.

**What are the types of fire extinguishers? And what is the proper way to use them?**

Fire extinguishers are classified into different types based on the classes of fires they are designed to combat. The classes of fires are categorized as follows:

Class A: Ordinary Combustibles

Fires involving ordinary combustible materials such as wood, paper, cloth, and some plastics.

Class B: Flammable Liquids

Fires involving flammable liquids, oils, greases, gases, and oil-based paints.

Class C: Electrical Equipment

Fires involving energized electrical equipment. It is crucial to use a non-conductive extinguishing agent to avoid electrical shock.

Class D: Combustible Metals

Fires involving combustible metals, such as magnesium, titanium, or sodium. Specialized extinguishing agents are required for these fires.

Class K: Cooking Oils and Fats

Fires involving cooking oils and fats typically found in kitchens. Class K extinguishers are designed for commercial kitchens.

Types of Fire Extinguishers:

Water (Class A):

Suitable for Class A fires involving ordinary combustibles. Not for use on flammable liquid or electrical fires.

Foam (Class A and B):

Effective on Class A and Class B fires. Forms a film on the surface of flammable liquids, preventing vapor release.

Carbon Dioxide (CO2) (Class B and C):

Suitable for Class B and Class C fires. Works by displacing oxygen, smothering the fire. Effective on electrical fires.

Dry Chemical (Class A, B, and C):

Versatile and effective on Class A, Class B, and Class C fires. Available in different types: monoammonium phosphate, sodium bicarbonate, or potassium bicarbonate.

Wet Chemical (Class K):

Specifically designed for Class K fires involving cooking oils and fats. Often used in commercial kitchens.

Dry Powder (Class D):

Designed for Class D fires involving combustible metals. Different types of dry powder extinguishers are suitable for specific metal fires.

Proper Way to Use a Fire Extinguisher (P.A.S.S. Method):

Remember the acronym P.A.S.S. to properly use a fire extinguisher:

Pull:

Pull the pin to break the seal and unlock the operating lever.

Aim:

Aim the nozzle or hose at the base of the fire. Do not aim at the flames; aim at the source of the fire.

Squeeze:

Squeeze the operating lever to discharge the extinguishing agent.

Sweep:

Sweep from side to side, covering the entire base of the fire, until the flames are extinguished. Keep a safe distance and be prepared for re-ignition.

Additional Tips:

Know the Fire Extinguisher's Limitations:

Ensure you are using the correct type of extinguisher for the fire class. Using the wrong type may be ineffective or even dangerous.

Maintain a Safe Distance:

Stand at a safe distance from the fire and approach it cautiously. Do not compromise your safety.

Have an Escape Route:

Always have an escape route behind you. If the fire cannot be controlled, evacuate immediately.

Call for Help:

Even if you manage to control the fire, call emergency services to ensure professional help is on the way.

Regular Inspections:

Regularly inspect and maintain your fire extinguishers to ensure they are in proper working condition.

Training:

Familiarize yourself and others with the location and proper use of fire extinguishers. Training can enhance response effectiveness.

Always prioritize safety, and if you have any doubts about using a fire extinguisher, evacuate the area and call for professional assistance.

## Let's pack a bug-out bag! What should be in it?

A bug-out bag, also known as an emergency go-bag or 72-hour kit, is a portable kit that contains essential items to help you survive for up to 72 hours in case of an emergency or evacuation. Here's a comprehensive list of items to consider including in your bug-out bag:

Basic Essentials:

Backpack:

A durable and comfortable backpack to carry your essentials.

Water:

At least one gallon of water per person per day for a minimum of three days.

Non-Perishable Food:

Ready-to-eat or easy-to-prepare foods with a long shelf life, such as energy bars, canned goods, or freeze-dried meals.

Manual Can Opener:

If including canned goods in your kit.

Multi-Tool or Knife:

A versatile tool for various tasks.

First Aid Kit:

Bandages, antiseptic wipes, pain relievers, prescription medications, and other basic medical supplies.

Medications:

A supply of essential prescription medications.

Emergency Blanket:

Reflective or thermal blankets for warmth.

Clothing and Shelter:

Change of Clothes:

Extra socks, underwear, and weather-appropriate clothing.

Rain Gear:

Poncho or lightweight rain jacket.

Hat and Gloves:

Protect yourself from the elements.

Emergency Shelter:

Lightweight tent, tarp, or space blanket.

Tools and Lighting:

Flashlight:

With extra batteries or a hand-crank option.

Glow Sticks:

Provides low-level lighting for visibility.

Candles:

Long-burning candles for warmth and light.

Duct Tape:

A versatile tool for repairs.

Multi-Tool or Knife:

A versatile tool for various tasks.

Communication and Navigation:

Whistle:

For signaling and attracting attention.

Compass:

For navigation.

Map:

Local and regional maps of the area.

Notepad and Pen:

For jotting down information.

Hygiene and Sanitation:

Personal Hygiene Items:

Toothbrush, toothpaste, soap, and other toiletries.

Hand Sanitizer:

Maintain hygiene when water is scarce.

Tissues or Wet Wipes:

For personal hygiene.

Personal and Important Documents:

Identification:

Copies of important documents such as identification, insurance policies, medical records, and contact information.

Cash:

Small denominations for emergency use.

Additional Items:

Entertainment:

Books, cards, or other items for leisure.

Local Contact Information:

Emergency contact numbers and local information.

Portable Charger:

For charging essential electronic devices.

Fire Starter:

Waterproof matches or a fire starter tool.

Face Mask:

Especially relevant during health emergencies.

Self-Defense Items:

Personal safety items such as a whistle, pepper spray, or a small flashlight.

Considerations:

Personal Needs:

Customize your bug-out bag based on the specific needs of your family members, including infants, elderly individuals, or individuals with special medical needs.

Seasonal Considerations:

Adjust your clothing and gear based on the season and the specific climate of your region.

Regular Maintenance:

Periodically check and update the contents of your bug-out bag to ensure everything is in good condition and within expiration dates.

Weight Considerations:

Keep in mind that you may need to carry the bag for an extended period, so consider weight when packing.

Remember that this list is a starting point, and you should tailor your bug-out bag to meet your individual needs and the specific risks in your area. Regularly review and update your bag to ensure that the contents remain relevant and in good condition.

**For long-term prepping, should you grow a garden? What should you plant? How to use buckets to grow plants and how do you build a raised garden bed?**

Growing a garden is a valuable and sustainable aspect of long-term prepping. It provides a renewable source of fresh produce, enhances self-sufficiency, and contributes to overall resilience. Here are guidelines on what to plant, how to use buckets for container gardening, and how to build a raised garden bed:

What to Plant:

Vegetables:

Choose a variety of vegetables that are well-suited to your climate and soil conditions. Common choices include tomatoes, peppers, lettuce, carrots, beans, and squash.

Herbs:

Plant herbs like basil, mint, oregano, and rosemary for culinary and medicinal purposes.

Fruits:

If space allows, consider planting fruit-bearing trees or bushes such as apples, berries, or citrus fruits.

Root Vegetables:

Include root vegetables like potatoes, onions, and garlic for long-term storage.

Leafy Greens:

Grow leafy greens like spinach, kale, and Swiss chard for a continuous harvest.

Medicinal Plants:

Consider cultivating medicinal plants like aloe vera, chamomile, or echinacea.

Companion Plants:

Use companion planting strategies to enhance growth and deter pests. For example, planting marigolds can help deter nematodes.

Container Gardening with Buckets:

Container gardening is a space-efficient way to grow plants, and buckets can be repurposed for this purpose. Here's how to use buckets for container gardening:

Drainage:

Ensure that each bucket has drainage holes at the bottom to prevent waterlogging. Elevate the bucket slightly to allow excess water to drain.

Soil:

Use a high-quality potting mix or a combination of garden soil, compost, and perlite for good drainage.

Planting:

Follow the planting guidelines for each specific plant. Ensure proper spacing and depth.

Watering:

Water consistently and adjust the frequency based on the needs of the plants. Containers may dry out faster than in-ground plantings.

Sunlight:

Place the buckets in an area that receives adequate sunlight based on the plants' requirements.

Fertilization:

Use a balanced, water-soluble fertilizer according to the recommended application rates.

Building a Raised Garden Bed:

Raised garden beds offer several benefits, including improved soil drainage, better control over soil composition, and easier maintenance. Here's how to build a raised garden bed:

Materials:

Choose durable, rot-resistant materials such as cedar or redwood. Avoid treated wood that may leach harmful chemicals into the soil.

Size and Height:

Determine the size and height of the raised bed based on your available space and the types of plants you want to grow. Aim for a width that allows easy reach from either side.

Location:

Select a location that receives adequate sunlight for the plants you plan to grow.

Assembly:

Assemble the raised bed by connecting the pieces of wood to form a rectangular or square shape. Secure the corners with screws or bolts.

Lining:

Optionally, line the interior with landscaping fabric to prevent weeds from growing into the bed.

Soil:

Fill the bed with a high-quality gardening mix or a combination of garden soil, compost, and other amendments.

Planting:

Follow the planting guidelines for each specific plant. Raised beds allow for better organization and grouping of plants with similar needs.

Watering:

Provide consistent watering based on the needs of the plants. Raised beds may require more frequent watering than in-ground plantings.

Mulching:

Apply a layer of organic mulch to help retain soil moisture and suppress weeds.

Maintenance:

Regularly check for pests, diseases, and nutrient deficiencies. Raised beds are generally easier to maintain than traditional in-ground gardens.

Whether using containers, raised beds, or traditional in-ground methods, gardening can be a rewarding and sustainable practice. Consider the specific needs of the plants you choose to grow and adapt your gardening approach accordingly. Regular care, proper watering, and attention to soil health contribute to successful long-term gardening.

## For long-term prepping what essentials should you consider stockpiling?

For long-term prepping, it's important to stockpile essentials that can sustain you and your family in various scenarios, including natural disasters, economic disruptions, or other emergencies. Here's a comprehensive list of essential items to consider stockpiling:

Food and Water:

Water:

Aim for at least one gallon of water per person per day for a minimum of three days. Consider water purification methods or tools.

Non-Perishable Food:

Stock canned goods, dry goods, and non-perishable items with a long shelf life. Include items like rice, pasta, beans, canned vegetables, and canned proteins.

Snacks:

Include snacks like energy bars, nuts, dried fruits, and crackers for quick and easy consumption.

Food Preservation:

Consider long-term food storage options such as freeze-dried meals, dehydrated foods, and vacuum-sealed items.

Seeds:

Non-hybrid seeds for growing your own vegetables and herbs.

Medical Supplies:

First Aid Kit:

Bandages, antiseptic wipes, pain relievers, prescription medications, and other basic medical supplies.

Prescription Medications:

Stock an extra supply of essential prescription medications for chronic conditions.

Over-the-Counter Medications:

Include common medications for pain, fever, allergies, and stomach issues.

Hygiene and Sanitation:

Personal Hygiene Products:

Toothpaste, soap, shampoo, and other personal care items.

Sanitation Supplies:

Toilet paper, hand sanitizer, wet wipes, and garbage bags.

Clothing and Bedding:

Clothing:

Durable and weather-appropriate clothing, including extra socks, underwear, and outerwear.

Blankets and Sleeping Bags:

Provides warmth and comfort in case of power outages or displacement.

Shelter and Tools:

Tarp and Plastic Sheeting:

Useful for emergency shelter or covering damaged areas.

Multi-Tool:

A versatile tool for various tasks.

Lighting and Communication:

Flashlights and Batteries:

Ensure you have reliable sources of light.

Battery-Powered or Hand-Crank Radio:

Stay informed about the latest developments and emergency alerts.

Cooking and Food Preparation:

Portable Stove or Camp Cookware:

Allows for cooking without relying on electricity.

Manual Can Opener:

Essential for accessing canned goods.

Financial and Important Documents:

Cash:

Have some cash on hand in case of power outages or electronic payment system failures.

Important Documents:

Copies of important documents such as identification, insurance policies, and medical records in a waterproof container.

Tools and Equipment:

Multi-Tool or Knife:

A versatile tool for various tasks.

Fire Starter:

Waterproof matches or a fire starter tool.

Duct Tape:

A versatile tool for repairs.

Fuel and Energy:

Batteries:

Stockpile extra batteries for flashlights and other devices.

Fuel:

Store fuel for generators, stoves, or other essential equipment.

Gardening and Self-Sufficiency:

Gardening Supplies:

Seeds, gardening tools, and soil amendments for growing your own food.

Livestock and Animal Care:

If applicable, consider stockpiling food and supplies for pets or livestock.

Security and Defense:

Self-Defense Items:

Personal safety items such as a whistle, pepper spray, or a small flashlight.

Protective Gear:

Gloves, masks, and other protective gear.

Miscellaneous:

Entertainment and Comfort Items:

Books, games, or other items to keep spirits up during challenging times.

Local Contact Information:

Emergency contact numbers and local information.

Portable Charger:

For charging essential electronic devices.

Face Masks:

Especially relevant during health emergencies.

Cleaning Supplies:

Disinfectants, cleaning agents, and garbage bags.

Remember to regularly check and rotate stockpiled items to ensure they remain within expiration dates. Customize your stockpile based on your family size, specific needs, and any unique circumstances in your area. Additionally, consider creating a family emergency plan and staying informed about potential risks in your region.

**How do you collect rain water? Should you invest in water barrels?**

Collecting rainwater is a sustainable practice that can provide you with an additional source of water for various uses, such as watering plants, flushing toilets, or even for emergency drinking water. Investing in water barrels, also known as rain barrels or water tanks, is a practical way to store and manage collected rainwater. Here's a guide on how to collect rainwater and the benefits of using water barrels:

How to Collect Rainwater:

Install Gutters:

If your home doesn't already have gutters, install them to direct rainwater from the roof to a specific collection point.

Choose a Collection Surface:

Position the rain barrel under a downspout or a roof area where rainwater can be efficiently collected.

Install a Filter:

Attach a filter at the top of the downspout or over the opening of the rain barrel to prevent debris, leaves, and other contaminants from entering the barrel.

Elevate the Barrel:

Place the rain barrel on a stable and elevated surface to allow gravity flow. This elevation helps create pressure when using the collected water.

Use a Diverter System:

Consider installing a diverter system that automatically directs excess water away from the barrel once it's full. This prevents overflow and potential water damage.

Regular Maintenance:

Clean the filter and inspect the barrel regularly to ensure it is free of debris and contaminants.

Benefits of Using Water Barrels:

Conservation of Water:

Rain barrels allow you to collect and store rainwater, reducing the demand on municipal water supplies and lowering your water bills.

Sustainable Gardening:

Use collected rainwater for watering plants, gardens, and lawns, providing a natural and chlorine-free water source.

Emergency Water Supply:

In emergency situations or during water shortages, stored rainwater can serve as a backup water supply for drinking and household needs.

Reduction of Stormwater Runoff:

Collecting rainwater helps reduce stormwater runoff, which can carry pollutants into rivers and streams. This is particularly beneficial for the environment.

Watering Indoor Plants:

Use rainwater for indoor plants, reducing the need for tap water.

Cost Savings:

Over time, using rainwater can lead to cost savings on water bills.

Choosing the Right Water Barrels:

Material:

Water barrels are often made of plastic, wood, or metal. Plastic barrels are lightweight and resistant to corrosion. Choose a material that suits your preferences and local climate.

Capacity:

Consider the size of your property and your water needs when choosing the capacity of the water barrel. Barrels typically range from 50 to 100 gallons or more.

Cover and Seal:

Ensure the barrel has a secure cover and a tight seal to prevent mosquito breeding, algae growth, and contamination.

Overflow System:

Look for a barrel with an overflow system to prevent water damage when the barrel is full.

Durability:

Choose a durable and UV-resistant barrel that can withstand outdoor conditions.

Investing in water barrels is a practical and environmentally friendly way to harness the benefits of rainwater. It contributes to water conservation efforts and provides a sustainable water source for various purposes.

**Should you stockpile on bleach for purifying water? What is the ratio bleach to water?**

Stockpiling bleach for water purification is a practical and cost-effective approach for emergency preparedness. Bleach can be used to disinfect water and make it safe for drinking by killing or inactivating harmful microorganisms. When using bleach for water purification, it's crucial to follow proper guidelines to ensure effectiveness and safety. Here are recommendations for using bleach to purify water:

Bleach Concentration and Water Purification:

Type of Bleach:

Use regular, unscented household bleach without additives or additional ingredients. Do not use bleach with added fragrances, thickeners, or other chemicals.

Bleach Concentration:

The recommended concentration of bleach for water purification is typically 6% sodium hypochlorite. Check the label to confirm the bleach concentration.

Ratio of Bleach to Water:

The recommended ratio of bleach to water varies based on the water's clarity and the specific concentration of the bleach. Here are general guidelines:

Clear Water:

Use 8 drops of bleach per gallon of clear water.

Cloudy or Turbid Water:

Use 16 drops of bleach per gallon of cloudy or turbid water.

Mixing and Waiting:

Mix the bleach thoroughly with the water and wait for at least 30 minutes before consuming the treated water.

Step-by-Step Water Purification with Bleach:

Filter or Settle:

If the water is cloudy or turbid, filter it through a clean cloth or allow it to settle to remove sediment before adding bleach.

Add Bleach:

Add the appropriate number of drops of bleach to the water based on its clarity, as mentioned above.

Stir or Shake:

Mix the water and bleach thoroughly. If using a container with a lid, secure the lid and shake the container to distribute the bleach evenly.

Wait:

Allow the treated water to sit for at least 30 minutes. This waiting period is essential to ensure that the bleach has sufficient time to disinfect the water.

Smell Test:

After waiting, check the water for a slight chlorine smell. If you don't detect any chlorine odor, repeat the dosage and wait for an additional 15 minutes.

Taste Test:

The treated water should have a mild chlorine taste. If it doesn't, repeat the dosage and wait for an additional 15 minutes.

Storage:

Store the treated water in clean, food-grade containers with tight-fitting lids.

Cautionary Notes:

Bleach Expiration:

Check the expiration date on the bleach container, and replace it if it has expired. Expired bleach may lose its effectiveness.

Bleach Smell and Taste:

If the treated water has a strong chlorine smell or taste, it's an indication of excess bleach. Let the water stand uncovered for a while to allow the chlorine to dissipate or aerate the water by pouring it between clean containers.

Use Unscented Bleach:

Scented bleaches may contain additional chemicals that are not suitable for water purification.

Consult Local Health Authorities:

In certain situations, local health authorities may provide specific guidelines for water purification during emergencies. Follow their recommendations when available.

Bleach is an effective and readily available water purification method, but it's important to use it correctly and within recommended guidelines to ensure the safety of the treated water.

**What are some ways to defend your home? Can you make traps? What kind of traps?**

Defending your home involves a combination of physical security measures, strategic planning, and, in some cases, basic survival skills. While the idea of making traps might seem like something out of a movie, it's essential to approach home defense with a focus on legal and ethical considerations. Here are some practical and legal ways to enhance home defense:

Physical Security Measures:

Secure Doors and Windows:

Install solid doors with strong frames and secure locks. Reinforce windows with laminated glass or security film.

Outdoor Lighting:

Install motion-activated outdoor lighting to deter potential intruders and improve visibility around your property.

Fencing:

Use fences to define property boundaries and discourage unauthorized access. Consider sturdy, difficult-to-climb fencing.

Security Cameras:

Install security cameras to monitor entrances and vulnerable areas. Visible cameras can act as a deterrent.

Alarm Systems:

Use a monitored or unmonitored alarm system to alert you to potential threats. Display signs indicating the presence of an alarm.

Safe Room:

Designate a safe room within your home where you can retreat in case of an intruder. Reinforce the door and have communication devices inside.

Legal Considerations:

Local Laws:

Familiarize yourself with local laws regarding self-defense and home protection. Know when the use of force is legally justified.

Firearms:

If legally allowed and after proper training, consider firearms for home defense. Store them securely, follow safety guidelines, and comply with local laws.

Training:

If you choose to have firearms, seek proper training in their use and practice responsible gun ownership.

Non-Lethal Defense Options:

Pepper Spray:

Keep pepper spray or other non-lethal deterrents in easily accessible locations.

Security Signage:

Display signs indicating the presence of a security system, even if you don't have one. The appearance of security can deter potential threats.

Survival and Strategic Planning:

Emergency Supplies:

Have emergency supplies, including food, water, and medical kits, stored in a secure location.

Communication Plan:

Develop a communication plan with family members or neighbors in case of an emergency.

Neighborhood Watch:

Participate in or establish a neighborhood watch program to collaborate with neighbors on security.

Legal and Ethical Considerations for Traps:

Legal Consequences:

Creating traps that cause harm to individuals may have serious legal consequences. It's crucial to ensure that any measures taken comply with local laws.

Home Security Companies:

Consider consulting with professional home security companies for advice and assistance. They can provide legal and effective solutions.

Non-Lethal Deterrents:

Focus on non-lethal deterrents and legal security measures rather than creating potentially harmful traps.

It's important to strike a balance between securing your home and ensuring the safety of occupants and potential visitors. Legal and ethical considerations should guide your decisions when implementing home defense measures. Consulting with security professionals and local law enforcement can provide valuable insights into effective and lawful home defense strategies.


### What farm animals should I consider when becoming a prepper?

When considering farm animals as part of your prepping strategy, it's essential to choose animals that align with your goals, resources, and the specific conditions of your location. Here are some farm animals commonly considered by preppers, along with factors to consider:


Chickens:

Benefits:

Provide a consistent source of eggs and meat.

Excellent for pest control as they eat insects.

Can be raised in smaller spaces.

Considerations:

Requires secure coop and fencing.

Regular care for health and hygiene.

Goats:

Benefits:

Produce milk for dairy products.

Efficient at clearing vegetation.

Can be raised for meat.

Considerations:

Requires proper fencing.

Daily care, including feeding and milking.

Sheep:

Benefits:

Produce wool, milk, and meat.

Grazers that can help manage pasture.

Generally docile and easy to handle.

Considerations:

Requires proper fencing.

Regular care for health and shearing.

Rabbits:

Benefits:

High reproductive rate.

Provide lean meat.

Require less space compared to larger animals.

Considerations:

Need secure hutches.

Regular feeding and care.

Bees:

Benefits:

Produce honey and beeswax.

Essential for pollination in gardens.

Considerations:

Requires knowledge of beekeeping.

Proper safety equipment is essential.

Pigs:

Benefits:

Efficient at converting food to meat.

Can be raised on a variety of diets.

Useful for tilling and clearing land.

Considerations:

Require strong fencing.

Proper waste management.

Ducks and Geese:

Benefits:

Provide eggs and meat.

Efficient foragers.

Pest control in gardens and ponds.

Considerations:

Need access to water.

Proper housing and protection.

Cattle:

Benefits:

Produce milk and meat.

Can provide draft power for plowing.

Grazing helps manage pastures.

Considerations:

Require ample grazing space.

Proper fencing and handling facilities.

Llamas or Alpacas:

Benefits:

Produce fiber (wool).

Can be effective guard animals for other livestock.

Considerations:

Need proper care for fiber production.

Require secure fencing.

Considerations for All Livestock:

Space and Zoning:

Ensure you have enough space and comply with local zoning regulations.

Feed and Nutrition:

Understand the nutritional needs of each animal and have a reliable source of feed.

Healthcare:

Develop a plan for regular veterinary care and disease prevention.

Water Source:

Ensure access to a clean and reliable water source for all animals.

Waste Management:

Plan for proper waste disposal and manure management.

Climate Considerations:

Choose animals that are well-suited to your climate.

Before introducing farm animals, it's crucial to research and gain practical experience in their care. Consider the time, effort, and resources required for each type of livestock. Additionally, think about your goals, such as self-sufficiency, food production, or sustainability, and tailor your choice of animals accordingly. Consulting with local agricultural extension services or experienced farmers in your area can provide valuable insights and guidance.

**How do you correctly butcher a pigs and cows?**

Butchering a pig or cow is a complex process that requires knowledge, skill, and the right tools. If you're considering this, it's highly recommended to seek hands-on training or assistance from someone experienced in animal butchering. The following overview provides a general idea, but detailed guidance and practical experience are essential:

Butchering a Pig:

Tools Needed:

Sharp Knives:

Different knives for various cuts, such as a boning knife and a butcher knife.

Handsaw:

For splitting the carcass.

Meat Grinder:

For processing ground meat.

Cleaver:

For cutting through bones.

Steps:

Preparation:

Ensure the pig is properly restrained and has been slaughtered humanely.

Scalding and Scraping:

Scald the pig in hot water to loosen the hair, and then scrape the hair off.

Gutting:

Remove the internal organs carefully. Save the liver, heart, and other organs if desired.

Splitting:

Use a handsaw to split the carcass down the middle.

Hanging:

Hang the halves for further processing.

Quartering:

Quarter the carcass by cutting along the spine.

Primal Cuts:

Further divide the quarters into primal cuts (shoulder, loin, belly, ham).

Trimming and Deboning:

Trim excess fat and skin, and debone as needed for specific cuts.

Cutting to Preference:

Cut into individual cuts like chops, roasts, and ribs based on preference.

Grinding:

If making ground meat, use a meat grinder for the desired grind.

Butchering a Cow:

Tools Needed:

Sharp Knives:

Different knives for various cuts, including a boning knife and a butcher knife.

Handsaw or Bandsaw:

For cutting through bones.

Meat Grinder:

For processing ground meat.

Cleaver:

For heavy-duty cutting through bones.

Steps:

Preparation:

Ensure the cow is properly restrained and has been humanely slaughtered.

Hanging:

Hang the cow for easier processing.

Skinning:

Skin the carcass carefully.

Gutting:

Remove internal organs, saving any desired parts.

Splitting:

Use a handsaw or bandsaw to split the carcass down the middle.

Quartering:

Quarter the carcass by cutting along the spine.

Primal Cuts:

Further divide the quarters into primal cuts (forequarter and hindquarter).

Trimming and Deboning:

Trim excess fat and debone as needed for specific cuts.

Cutting to Preference:

Cut into individual cuts such as steaks, roasts, and ribs based on preference.

Grinding:

Use a meat grinder if making ground beef.

Safety Considerations:

Keep Tools Sharp:

Sharp tools are safer and make the butchering process more efficient.

Proper Handling:

Practice proper handling and sanitation to prevent contamination.

Hygiene:

Wash hands and tools regularly to maintain hygiene.

Eye and Hand Protection:

Consider wearing protective gear, including gloves and eye protection.

Cold Environment:

Work in a cool environment to maintain the quality of the meat.

It's crucial to emphasize that this overview is not a substitute for hands-on training or guidance from an experienced butcher. If you're new to butchering, consider seeking assistance or training from local experts, agricultural extension services, or butchering workshops. Always adhere to local regulations regarding the processing and handling of meat.

**How do you build a bee box and gather bees?**

Building a bee box, also known as a beehive or apiary, involves creating a structure that provides a suitable habitat for honey bees. Additionally, acquiring bees typically involves purchasing a package of bees or obtaining a bee swarm. Here's a basic guide on building a simple bee box and gathering bees:

Building a Bee Box (Langstroth Hive):

Materials Needed:

Wooden Components:

Hive boxes (deep, medium, and shallow).

Inner and outer covers.

Bottom board.

Frames for holding comb.

Tools:

Saw.

Hammer or nail gun.

Nails or screws.

Wood glue.

Hive tool for beekeeping.

Steps:

Assemble the Hive Boxes:

Construct the deep, medium, and shallow hive boxes. Ensure they have handholds for easy lifting.

Build Frames:

Assemble frames for each box using wooden frame components. Install foundation wax or plastic in the frames for the bees to build comb.

Assemble the Bottom Board:

Construct the bottom board, which serves as the base of the hive. It can have an entrance reducer for controlling hive access.

Construct Inner and Outer Covers:

Build inner and outer covers. The inner cover typically has a central hole for ventilation, while the outer cover provides protection from the elements.

Paint or Seal:

Paint or seal the exterior of the boxes to protect them from weathering.

Add Hive Stand (Optional):

Consider adding a hive stand to elevate the hive and provide additional ventilation.

Gathering Bees:

Option 1: Purchase a Package of Bees

Source a Bee Package:

Contact local beekeeping suppliers or associations to purchase a package of bees. A package usually includes a queen and worker bees.

Install Bees in the Hive:

Install the bees in the hive by shaking them from the package into the hive. Follow the instructions provided by the supplier.

Feed the Bees:

Provide sugar syrup to the bees to help them establish their hive.

Option 2: Capture a Swarm

Prepare a Hive Box:

Set up a bait hive with frames and a small entrance to attract a swarm.

Monitor for Swarms:

Keep an eye on local bee activity, especially during swarm season. Swarms may settle on a branch or other surface before moving into a hive.

Capture the Swarm:

If you observe a swarm, carefully capture it using a swarm box or by shaking the bees into your prepared hive.

Provide a Hive:

Transfer the captured swarm into a prepared hive box. Ensure they have sufficient food and resources.

General Beekeeping Tips:

Protective Gear:

Wear a bee suit, gloves, and a veil to protect yourself from stings.

Learn Beekeeping Basics:

Educate yourself on basic beekeeping practices, including hive inspection, pest management, and honey extraction.

Join a Beekeeping Association:

Consider joining a local beekeeping association to connect with experienced beekeepers and gain valuable insights.

Regular Hive Inspections:

Conduct regular hive inspections to ensure the health and productivity of your bee colony.

Remember, beekeeping requires ongoing care and attention. Bees play a crucial role in pollination and honey production, and responsible beekeeping practices are essential for their well-being. If you are new to beekeeping, consider seeking guidance from experienced beekeepers or taking a beekeeping course to enhance your skills and knowledge.

**How do you properly butcher a chicken?**

Butchering a chicken involves several steps to process the bird for consumption. Before attempting to butcher a chicken, it's essential to understand the process, have the right tools, and practice good hygiene. Here's a basic guide on how to properly butcher a chicken:

Tools Needed:

Killing Cone or Restraining Device:

A killing cone is a commonly used tool that restrains the chicken during the slaughter process.

Sharp Knife:

A sharp, sturdy knife is necessary for efficient and humane processing.

Scalding Pot:

A pot of hot water for scalding the chicken to facilitate feather removal.

Plucking Machine or Plucking Fingers:

A plucking machine or plucking fingers (rubberized fingers on a drill) for feather removal.

Cleaning and Evisceration Tools:

Gutting scissors or a sharp knife for evisceration.

Containers for organs and waste.

Water Hose:

A hose for cleaning and rinsing the chicken.

Steps:

Prepare the Work Area:

Set up a clean and organized workspace with all the necessary tools.

Humanely Restrain the Chicken:

Use a killing cone or another humane restraining device to calm and immobilize the chicken.

Make the Kill Cut:

Use a sharp knife to make a quick and humane cut across the chicken's throat, severing the carotid arteries. Ensure a swift and clean cut for humane euthanasia.

Hang and Bleed:

Hang the chicken upside down to allow the blood to drain from the carcass. Ensure the bleeding process is complete before moving to the next step.

Scalding:

Immerse the chicken in hot water (around 145-150°F or 63-66°C) for about 45 seconds to loosen the feathers. The water temperature and duration may vary based on the size of the chicken.

Plucking:

Pluck the feathers from the chicken. Use a plucking machine or plucking fingers for efficient feather removal. Begin with larger feathers and move to smaller ones.

Remove Head and Feet:

Cut off the head and feet using a sharp knife. Discard or save them for stock if desired.

Evisceration (Gutting):

Make an incision from the vent up to the chest. Carefully open the body cavity and remove the internal organs, including the crop, gizzard, liver, heart, and lungs.

Clean and Rinse:

Rinse the chicken thoroughly with clean water to remove any remaining blood or debris.

Inspect and Chill:

Inspect the chicken for any remaining feathers or unwanted parts. Chill the chicken in a refrigerator or with ice packs to cool the meat quickly.

Packaging:

Once chilled, package the chicken for storage or further processing.

Hygiene and Safety:

Personal Hygiene:

Wash hands and tools regularly during the process to maintain hygiene.

Proper Disposal:

Dispose of waste in a responsible manner, considering local regulations.

Use a Sharp Knife:

A sharp knife ensures a quick and humane kill and makes the process more efficient.

Humane Treatment:

Practice humane and ethical treatment throughout the butchering process.

Remember, butchering animals requires practice, and it's crucial to approach the process with respect and consideration for the well-being of the animals. If you are new to chicken butchering, consider seeking guidance from experienced individuals or participating in a local workshop to gain hands-on experience. Additionally, always adhere to local regulations regarding the processing of poultry.

**How do you butcher a deer?**

Butchering a deer involves several steps to process the carcass into manageable cuts for consumption. Proper field dressing and processing techniques are essential to ensure the quality and safety of the meat. Here's a general guide on how to butcher a deer:

Tools Needed:

Sharp Knives:

A sturdy knife for initial cuts and skinning.

A boning knife for detailed work.

A saw for cutting through bones.

Game Bags or Plastic Bags:

To protect the meat and allow air circulation.

Hanging System:

A system for hanging the deer during butchering, such as gambrels and pulleys.

Cooler or Refrigeration:

Adequate refrigeration or cooler space for storing the meat.

Steps:

Field Dressing:

Field dress the deer as soon as possible after harvesting to cool the meat and prevent spoilage.

Make a shallow cut around the anus and genitals, being careful not to puncture the intestines.

Cut through the skin from the chest to the base of the neck.

Carefully cut around the windpipe and food pipe, and then cut through the diaphragm to free the organs from the chest cavity.

Pull the organs out of the body cavity, allowing the deer to cool.

Transport to Butchering Site:

Transport the deer to a location suitable for butchering, ideally a clean and cool area.

Hanging the Deer:

Hang the deer by the hind legs using a hanging system. This makes it easier to access and process different cuts.

Skinning:

Make a cut from the hind legs to the neck along the inside of each leg.

Peel the skin away from the body using your hands or a knife.

Remove the head and neck, and continue peeling the skin down to the front legs.

Quartering:

Use a saw to cut through the pelvic bone and spine to separate the hindquarters from the rest of the carcass.

Repeat the process to separate the front quarters.

The remaining torso can be further divided into the ribcage and backstraps.

Deboning:

Remove the backstraps along the spine using a boning knife.

Trim away the meat from the ribs and other bones.

Processing the Meat:

Trim the meat into desired cuts, such as roasts, steaks, and ground meat.

Package the meat in game bags or plastic bags for transportation or storage.

Cooling and Storage:

Ensure the meat is properly cooled and stored to prevent spoilage.

Consider aging the meat for a few days in a cool environment for improved tenderness.

Dispose of Remaining Parts:

Properly dispose of non-edible parts, such as organs and hide, in accordance with local regulations.

Safety Considerations:

Wear Protective Gear:

Wear gloves and other protective gear to prevent contamination.

Keep Tools Sharp:

Use sharp knives for efficient and safe butchering.

Hygiene:

Practice good hygiene throughout the butchering process to ensure food safety.

Proper Disposal:

Dispose of waste responsibly, adhering to local regulations.

If you're new to deer butchering, consider seeking guidance from experienced hunters or participating in a butchering workshop to gain hands-on experience. Additionally, always follow local regulations regarding hunting and processing game animals.

**How do you make a homemade fishing pole? How do you properly clean fish and filet them?**

Making a homemade fishing pole is a simple and practical skill, especially in survival or emergency situations. Here's a basic guide on how to make a makeshift fishing pole using readily available materials. Additionally, I'll provide steps on how to properly clean and fillet fish:

Homemade Fishing Pole:

Materials Needed:

Flexible Branch or Sapling:

Choose a flexible branch or sapling that is approximately 6 to 8 feet long.

Fishing Line:

Use a strong and lightweight fishing line. Dental floss can also be used in a pinch.

Hook:

Attach a fishing hook to the line. Hooks can be purchased or made from small pieces of wire.

Bait:

Use natural bait such as worms, insects, or small pieces of food.

Steps:

Select and Prepare the Branch:

Choose a flexible branch or sapling that is free from cracks or weaknesses.

Remove any side branches and leaves.

Attach the Fishing Line:

Tie one end of the fishing line securely to the tip of the branch.

Add the Hook:

Attach the fishing hook to the free end of the fishing line using a secure knot.

Bait the Hook:

Add bait to the hook. Ensure the bait is securely attached to withstand casting.

Test the Pole:

Gently test the flexibility and strength of the pole by flexing it slightly. Make adjustments as needed.

Fish:

Cast the line into the water and wait for a fish to bite.

Cleaning and Filleting Fish:

Tools Needed:

Sharp Fillet Knife:

Use a sharp, flexible fillet knife for precise cuts.

Cutting Board:

A stable surface for filleting fish.

Steps:

Scale the Fish (Optional):

If the fish has scales, use a scaling tool or the back of the knife to remove them. This step is optional for some fish species.

Remove the Head (Optional):

Cut behind the fish's gills to remove the head. This step is optional and depends on personal preference.

Make the Initial Incision:

Lay the fish on its side on the cutting board.

Make an incision just behind the pectoral fin and along the top of the fish toward the tail.

Separate the Fillet:

Use the fillet knife to separate the fillet from the spine. Glide the knife along the backbone, following the contours of the fish.

Repeat on the Other Side:

Flip the fish and repeat the process on the other side.

Skinning (Optional):

To remove the skin, make a small cut at the tail end of the fillet.

Hold the fillet with one hand and use the knife to carefully separate the flesh from the skin.

Remove Rib Bones:

Run the knife along the rib bones to remove them from the fillet.

Inspect for Bones:

Inspect the fillet for any remaining pin bones and remove them with tweezers.

Rinse and Store:

Rinse the fillets with clean water.

Store the fillets in a cooler or on ice until ready to cook.

Proper cleaning and filleting techniques vary slightly depending on the species of fish, so it's essential to adapt the process based on the fish you are handling. Practice makes perfect, so the more you clean and fillet fish, the more proficient you'll become.

**How do you make an emergency plan for it to be successful? Should it be written out and given to each member in your family?**

Creating a successful emergency plan is crucial for ensuring the safety and well-being of your family in times of crisis. A well-thought-out plan should cover various aspects of preparedness, communication, and evacuation. Here's a guide on how to create an effective emergency plan, and yes, having it written out and shared with each family member is a key component:

Steps to Create an Emergency Plan:

Identify Potential Risks:

Assess the types of emergencies that are likely to occur in your region, such as natural disasters (earthquakes, floods, hurricanes) or man-made incidents (fires, power outages, etc.).

Create a Communication Plan:

Establish a communication strategy that includes contact information for all family members.

Designate an out-of-town contact person who can serve as a central point for communication.

Assemble Emergency Kits:

Prepare emergency kits for each family member, including essentials like water, non-perishable food, first aid supplies, medications, important documents, and personal hygiene items.

Define Evacuation Routes:

Identify primary and alternative evacuation routes from your home and establish meeting points in case family members are separated.

Plan for Pets:

Include provisions for the care and evacuation of pets, including food, water, and transportation.

Learn Emergency Procedures:

Familiarize yourself and your family with emergency procedures relevant to the identified risks. This includes knowing how to turn off utilities, where emergency exits are located, and how to administer basic first aid.

Create a Shelter-in-Place Plan:

Establish procedures for sheltering in place if evacuation is not possible. Identify safe rooms and designate areas for different types of emergencies.

Document Important Information:

Compile and document essential information, including medical records, insurance policies, identification, and financial documents. Store copies in a waterproof container.

Assign Responsibilities:

Clearly assign responsibilities to each family member. This may include tasks such as grabbing specific items, helping younger family members, or assisting with pets.

Practice Regularly:

Conduct emergency drills with your family, including evacuation and shelter-in-place scenarios. Practice using emergency equipment and review evacuation routes.

Review and Update:

Regularly review and update your emergency plan to account for changes in family dynamics, contact information, and new information about potential risks.

Write It Down and Share:

Document the emergency plan in writing, ensuring it includes all relevant details. Make copies for each family member and distribute the plan. Consider having digital copies as well.

Components of a Written Emergency Plan:

Emergency Contacts:

Phone numbers and addresses for family members, neighbors, and emergency services.

Meeting Points:

Designated meeting points both within the neighborhood and outside of it.

Evacuation Routes:

Clear maps with primary and alternative evacuation routes marked.

Communication Plan:

Clear instructions on how and when to communicate during an emergency.

Emergency Kit Checklist:

A checklist of items to include in each family member's emergency kit.

Pet Plan:

Instructions and supplies for the care and evacuation of pets.

Medical Information:

Important medical information for each family member.

Shelter-in-Place Procedures:

Specific instructions for sheltering in place, including designated safe areas.

Responsibility Assignments:

A list of responsibilities assigned to each family member.

Emergency Procedures:

Step-by-step instructions for different emergency scenarios.

Sharing the written emergency plan with each family member ensures that everyone is on the same page and can act quickly and efficiently when needed. Regularly review and update the plan to account for any changes in your family, living situation, or the surrounding environment.

## What herbs can be used in place of medication?

While herbs have been used for centuries for various health purposes, it's important to note that herbal remedies should be approached with caution and in consultation with a healthcare professional. Some herbs may interact with medications or have side effects, and their efficacy can vary. Here are a few herbs that have been traditionally used for various health concerns, but it's crucial to consult with a healthcare provider before using them as substitutes for medications:

## 1. Turmeric:

Traditional Use: Anti-inflammatory, antioxidant.

Caution: May interact with blood-thinning medications.

## 2. Ginger:

Traditional Use: Anti-nausea, anti-inflammatory.

Caution: May interact with blood-thinning medications.

## 3. Garlic:

Traditional Use: Cardiovascular health, immune support.

Caution: May interact with blood-thinning medications.

## 4. Peppermint:

Traditional Use: Digestive issues, headaches.

Caution: May exacerbate heartburn in some individuals.

## 5. Chamomile:

Traditional Use: Relaxation, sleep aid, digestive support.

Caution: May cause allergic reactions in some individuals.

## 6. Echinacea:

Traditional Use: Immune support.

Caution: Not recommended for individuals with autoimmune disorders.

## 7. Lavender:

Traditional Use: Relaxation, sleep aid.

Caution: Ingestion may cause nausea; use in moderation.

## 8. Valerian:

Traditional Use: Sleep aid, anxiety.

Caution: May cause dizziness and drowsiness; avoid alcohol.

### 9. Ginseng:

Traditional Use: Energy, immune support.

Caution: May interact with certain medications; avoid in some health conditions.

### 10. St. John's Wort:

- **Traditional Use:** Mild to moderate depression.

- **Caution:** Interacts with various medications, including antidepressants.

Important Considerations:

Consult a Professional:

Always consult with a healthcare professional before using herbs, especially if you are taking medications or have underlying health conditions.

Quality Matters:

Choose high-quality, reputable sources for herbal supplements to ensure purity and potency.

Dosage and Duration:

Follow recommended dosages and guidelines for the specific herb you're using. Avoid prolonged use without professional guidance.

Be Aware of Interactions:

Some herbs may interact with medications. Inform your healthcare provider about all herbs and supplements you are taking.

Monitor for Side Effects:

Pay attention to any adverse reactions or side effects. Discontinue use if you experience unexpected symptoms.

Pregnancy and Lactation:

Some herbs may not be safe during pregnancy or breastfeeding. Seek guidance from a healthcare provider.

Remember, while herbs can offer complementary support for certain health concerns, they should not be viewed as replacements for prescribed medications or professional medical advice. Herbal remedies should be integrated into your healthcare plan with the guidance and supervision of a qualified healthcare provider.

**Summary:**

This book has covered a range of topics related to emergency preparedness and survival skills. It included discussions on food and water storage, first aid, communication devices, survival techniques, butchering animals, security measures, herbal alternatives to medications, creating a homemade fishing pole, and developing an effective emergency plan. The emphasis was on practical tips for self-sufficiency and safety in various scenarios.

www.ingramcontent.com/pod-product-compliance
Lightning Source LLC
Chambersburg PA
CBHW051210120626
46547CB00013B/1289